Education for alienation

Prentice-Hall International, Inc., *London*
Prentice-Hall of Australia, Pty. Ltd., *Sydney*
Prentice-Hall of Canada, Ltd., *Toronto*
Prentice-Hall of India (Private) Ltd., *New Delhi*
Prentice-Hall of Japan, Inc., *Tokyo*

Education for Alienation

NATHANIEL HICKERSON

Department of Social and Philosophical Foundations
School of Education
University of Southern California

PRENTICE-HALL, INC., Englewood Cliffs, N.J.

Preface

In our country today there is an enormous waste of human energy, resources, and talent. Great numbers of our people, the vast majority of whom have been born into poverty, do not fulfill their potential in ways useful to themselves and to society.

This book will be an attempt to show how our public schools, as mirrors of our society, have played a significant role in creating the conditions that have led to the waste of talent and ability and to the subsequent loss of dignity and self-worth on the part of millions of our citizens.

Contents

Education for alienation

ONE

Schools: mirrors of society

Public education in the United States is an instrument of American society. There is little evidence to support the contention by many leaders in professional education that public education in America is reconstructionist in nature; that is, that the public schools take the lead in effecting social change. In reality, history indicates that in all societies where public education developed, it has served as a reflector of the existing social order. Close scrutiny of the systems of public education functioning in different societies today reveals a clear relationship between the social and political framework upon which the society is built and the philosophic principles upon which its public education is formulated.

In the United States, examples of the relationship between the needs of the society and the procedures of the public school are to be found throughout the history of American education. For example, the early American "public schools" were opened for the purpose of providing religious

1

instruction for children. Located in Puritan New England, where concern with religious matters was dominant in the culture pattern of the society, these schools were established in 1647 by the General Court of Massachusetts for specific, well-defined reasons. Stated in the "Old Deluder Satan Act" is the following:

> It being one chief project of that old deluder, Satan, to keep men from the knowledge of the scriptures, as in former times, by keeping them in an unknown tongue, so in these latter times by persuading from the use of tongues, that so at least the true sense and meaning of the original might be clouded by false glosses of saint-seeming deceivers, that learning may not be buried in the grave of our fathers in church and commonwealth, the Lord assisting our endeavors.
>
> It is therefore ordered that every township in this jurisdiction, after the Lord hath increased them to the number of fifty householders, shall then forthwith appoint one within their town to teach all such children as shall resort to him to write and read, whose wages shall be paid either by the parents or masters of such children, or by the inhabitants in general, by way of supply, as the major part of those that order the prudentials of the town shall appoint.

By the turn of the twentieth century, millions of immigrants had come to the United States from Europe. At this time our public schools were faced with "Americanizing" and integrating the newcomers. Emphasis was placed not only on teaching the immigrant children to read and write English, but also on helping them to adapt to the American culture around them. William M. French says:

> The tremendous flood of persons from other countries, often without any traditions of democracy, posed a great challenge to American democracy. That these huge numbers became Americanized and assimilated into the general population is a great tribute to them and to American institu-

tions. Among these American institutions which made it possible to absorb so many people with diverse traditions and customs was the American public school. . . . [It] was largely the public school system which made the major contribution in this process both through educating the children of the immigrants and through Americanization and citizenship classes for the adults.[1]

Lawrence Cremin states:

> With the profound shift in the character of American immigration during the later years of the nineteenth century, this Americanizing function was again called to the fore.[2]

These children were encouraged to change their dress habits, hair styles, leisure-time activities, and a multitude of other characteristics that marked them as foreigners. Often the schools encountered opposition from the immigrant parents who saw the demise of their traditional culture in these efforts. America in 1900 needed Americans who thought, spoke, dressed, and acted like Americans. We gave to our schools a major part of the responsibility for effecting the transformation of the children's culture. How successful our schools were is exemplified by the classic American story of the conflict between the parents of the old country and the children of the new.

Also at the turn of the twentieth century our need for better-educated people brought about a rapid growth in the number of secondary schools over the land. The new industrial giant needed skilled and learned men and women to run the factories and offices, and to sell the products. We now required Americans who thought and acted in keeping with

[1] *America's Educational Tradition* (New York: D. C. Heath & Company, 1964), p. 304.
[2] *The Transformation of the Schools* (New York: Alfred A. Knopf, Inc., 1961), p. 66.

a new national image. Our public system of education responded almost automatically. Elementary school education was no longer enough. Public high schools, scarce and restricted in the nineteenth century, now began to spring up in thousands of American communities. Children in public schools were now expected to learn not only "readin'," "writin'," and "'rithmetic," but industrial arts, typing, shorthand, and similar skills. The emphasis in secondary schools was no longer on a narrow academic curriculum and an elite group of children. The high schools became "public" to answer the needs of the public. A broad new concept of curriculum developed to create the new kind of American needed to provide the manpower for a nation in transition from an agrarian land to an industrial complex. Society spoke, and the schools answered.

Since World War II, American society has found increasing need to develop anti-Communist citizens. Frequent representations—pictorial and written, as well as verbal, in all the communications media—are filled with material depicting the dangers of communism and are disseminated among our people. Public officials vie with each other to prove that they are more fervently anti-Communist than their opponents. Other prominent citizens, whose opinions are respected, also follow the same path.

The American public school has reacted with predictable speed to this requirement of American society. History textbooks disparage, and even distort, Soviet and Communist history. Many American children graduate from high school never having discussed in their classes the alliance between the United States and the Soviet Union during World War II. Social studies curricula minimize, and in many cases entirely ignore, the historical role of the early American Anarchists, Socialists, Syndicalists, and Communists in the development of the American trade-union movement. Such important events in American history as the Pullman strike, the Haymarket riots, Debs's imprisonment, the Palmer raids, and the Sacco-Vanzetti trial are scarcely mentioned in most secondary school history books. For example, one high school history text[3] in widespread use does not even have Anarchist, Socialist, or Syndicalist listed in the index. Eugene V. Debs is mentioned once, according to the index, and only then to note his arrest during the Pullman strike of 1894. There is no reference to his candidacy for President in 1920 when he polled nearly a million votes. About 100 words are devoted to the Haymarket Riot, but no mention is made of the protest voiced by intellectuals and others after the conviction of the Anarchists on charges of having incited riot. Neither Attorney General Palmer nor the Palmer Raids are listed in the index. There is no listing of the Sacco-Vanzetti trial, nor is there any mention of the International Workers of the World (I.W.W.) in the text dealing with labor unions.

Communists or suspected Communists are given short shrift in the overwhelming majority of American public schools. Indeed, as a contingent for employment as a public school teacher nearly every American state requires that a loyalty oath be signed denying Communist affiliation.

We have learned much about education in the Soviet Union in recent years, and it will be interesting to note how the public schools in another society also serve as the agent of the established social order. In the Soviet Union the same relationship between the needs of its society and public school procedure can be easily discerned. Herschel and Edith Alt write:

> How this singleness of purpose and community of effort influence the economic life is well known. What is not gen-

[3] Everett Augspurger and Richard A. McLemore, *Our Nation's Story* (River Forest, Ill.: Laidlaw Brothers, 1960).

erally understood is the manner in which the key principles
in family life and the patterns of child care and child education likewise derive from established national purpose. Soviet
concepts of personality, the basic principles of education, the
choice of psychological interpretation of human behavior as
well as theories of etiology and treatment of mental illness
are a few other examples of accommodation to a central
purpose.[4]

For example, there is great emphasis on teaching young children that survival of fatherland is dependent upon the willingness of each child to consider the needs of others, or of
the state, before his own. In this way Soviet authorities hope
to produce a people whose sense of duty to fatherland will
greatly diminish self-interest. Hence, where facilities are available, Russian children start their formal training at ages two
or three, for Soviet leaders feel that even at this early age the
formal process of orientation should begin.

Commenting on this over-all philosophical commitment
of considering the development of each individual child only
as it pertains to specific societal goals, the Alts state:

> The general observation was, however, that of course
> Soviet educators were very much concerned with individual
> development, and this would be followed by comments about
> the importance of the child's opportunity to choose his pro-
> fession, to develop his talents to the fullest extent. There
> seemed to be no understanding of our concept of the unique-
> ness of the individual and the premium we place upon the
> development of the individual personality as an end in itself.[5]

Dr. Anna Simson, Director of Research in the Children's
Division of Kashenka Psychiatric Hospital, Moscow, is quoted

[4] *Russia's Children* (New York: Bookman Associates, 1959), p.
70.

[5] *Ibid.*, p. 72.

as saying, "Our workers are interested in feelings, too, but feelings must be directed to a useful purpose." [6]

Dr. Spock, talking about Russian school and nursery personnel, states:

> They are proud of their contributions. They are unanimous about the qualities and ideals that are to be inculcated in children—industriousness, love of education, cooperativeness, dedication to children. The children sense the consistency that surrounds them, in both the adults and the other children. They accept this uniform guidance with relative ease.[7]

Commenting on the Alts's book, Dr. Spock says: What struck them most was the conforming, cooperative behavior of these children.[8]

In the Russian pre-school nurseries the children are encouraged to share everything that can be shared with the others, and are rewarded for their efforts. Subordination of individual wishes to the wishes of the group is continually stressed. Individual playpens are frowned upon, as are individual high chairs for eating. Instead, group play, group eating, and so on are practiced. Children are taught to avoid fighting or squabbling with each other, no matter what the provocation, and they are urged to take the role of mediator in disputes involving other children. It is not uncommon in Soviet nurseries to see four-year-old children remonstrating with their younger classmates for antisocial or overly aggressive behavior.

In these examples may be seen the close tie between the

[6] *Ibid.*, p. 73.
[7] Benjamin Spock, "Russian Children Don't Whine, Squabble, or Break Things—Why?" *The Ladies Home Journal*, October 1960, p. 33.
[8] *Ibid.*, p. 30.

present need of Soviet society, the creation of a highly social-oriented citizen, and the role of the public education institution whose task it is to give Soviet society what it demands.

Further on this point, Herschel and Edith Alt say:

> Love of country means loyalty and obedience to the regime and its leaders, excluding all other loyalties. Even though the child is taught to love and respect his parents, his primary loyalty is to the state. Loyalty within the family is acceptable only so long as the family's activities and attitudes are in harmony with the purposes of the state.
>
> While it is the duty of parents to protect and teach their child, this is a delegated responsibility, entrusted to them only so long as their efforts—always open to observation by neighbors, teachers, and other children—bring about the desired results.[9]

Again, in the Soviet Union, where profit for personal gain is considered inimical to the best interests of society and the individual, children in the schools are taught the evils of the profit system and are encouraged to devote their talents and energies to aiding their society by becoming good Socialist citizens, dedicated to improving the fatherland. Reward is given to those children who are best able to defend socialist antiprofit theory and to explain to others how socialist concepts and practices are supposedly leading the world to greater freedom and humaneness.

It is hard to conceive of a teacher in Soviet schools preaching "individualism" or advocating capitalism and free enterprise. Soviet schools are organized as surrogates of existing Soviet culture. The teacher is expected to abide by the state's needs in the education of the young. If he fails in this duty, he is replaced by one who will not fail.

In primitive societies, though the education process of

[9] *Op. cit.*, p. 78.

children is not usually formalized, it nonetheless centers around the needs of the extant society. Boys and girls in primitive groups need to grow up to become functioning men and women, as functioning is defined by their specific society. Imposed upon these children, therefore, is the learning they must acquire in order to survive as productive members of their group and in order to perpetuate the particular forms of their society. At an early age they are taught to hunt, make weapons, farm, weave, dance, or perform any other skills they have to know to be accepted into adulthood in their culture. They are taught religious rites and kinship regulations, and they learn how to avoid behavior that is taboo among their people. Although the process of education is usually through direct experience rather than from an artificial classroom situation, the results desired are the same: children must learn what the society wishes them to learn. It is inconceivable that children in one particular primitive society would be taught the customs, technology, and general culture of any other group. Any adult member of the society who proposed such a policy would be met with stern opposition and would find himself in conflict with the existing social order.

Thus, American society demands that its public schools reflect the character of its society; in Soviet society it is no different; primitive peoples do the same.

In American society there is a dominant culture, which has developed as a result of years of the sharing of common experiences. Needless to say, there are local variations of the culture pattern, but basic commitments commonly are to particular patterns of behavior in the dominant culture. The "common" culture to be transmitted by the public schools is therefore based upon a set of accepted commitments, understood all over our nation. These cultural beliefs and practices provide the stand upon which the institution of formal American education rests. Americans believe in freedom and democracy; free enterprise and capitalism; equal opportunity for all; relationship between effort and reward; the Golden Rule.

Since the schools everywhere in America are charged with the responsibility of transmitting these beliefs to the students, it would be expected that "common" techniques and methods would be developed to implement the dissemination of the "common" culture. In turn, these common techniques and methods require common philosophical assumptions. As our dominant culture is supposed to be unassailable, so are the assumptions made by our schools. As our culture may not be challenged except within rigidly defined limits, so may the philosophical assumptions on which our education rests not be challenged, except within the same kind of rigid limitations. These assumptions are the substance of American education. They are adhered to in Maine as in California; they are fundamentally the same everywhere in our country where public education is found. These assumptions are relatively few in number and easy to understand. Teacher-training institutions all over the country subscribe to them and build their programs around them. School boards accept these premises and construct the local school programs in such a way as to maintain continuous and harmonious identity with them. Superintendents, principals, counselors, and teachers carry out their share of the program based upon these assumptions. Indeed, the structure of American public education stands like a rock on this thin layer of intellectual and philosophical propositions: (1) native intelligence in children is measurable; (2) our devices used for measuring children's intelligence are sufficiently accurate to be relied upon; (3) only certain children are capable of academic education in depth; (4) children capable of academic education in depth can be identified, in the majority of cases, in the early years of elementary education; (5) program tracks other than the academic should be provided for children incapable of depth academic school work; (6) the school must help the student to adjust realistically to his abilities and potentialities as determined primarily by intelligence- and achievement-measuring tests and devices.

Although school districts may vary the structure, the components are remarkably uniform. There are few, if any, public school districts in the United States that operate under any other set of assumptions unless the district is so poor that it cannot afford the cost of obtaining devices and instruments necessary to put the program into operation. Such districts are generally regarded as having substandard educational opportunities for their children, and, indeed, are often referred to as medieval and barbaric.

It is necessary to examine the validity of this group of assumptions and the consequences that accrue from them. Equally important, we shall see how these assumptions fulfill the requirements of current American society, for we must not forget that these assumptions have been developed and sanctified as a result of the demands made by American society that its public schools reflect our present culture.

Not all modern societies accept the view that native intelligence is measurable. In fact in some societies, such as the Soviet Union, there is denial of differences of measurable potentialities among healthy children. According to the Alts:

> If psychological tests disclose differences and limitations in ability, then they have no place in educational practice because the belief in equal abilities and the educability of the average individual for the highest contribution to the state must be sustained.[10]

[10] *Op. cit.*, p. 70.

Russian educators and scientists hold that differences in performance by children in school may be traced either to environmental factors or to physical damage. The identical curriculum is given to nearly all children in grades one through seven in the Soviet schools. There are no preconceived assumptions or *a priori* decisions made about children's abilities. All children are expected to learn to read and to complete successfully the same courses of study, including eight years of Russian language; four years of literature (Pushkin, Chekhov, Dostoyevsky, Turgenev, Tolstoy, Gorky, etc.); eight years of mathematics, including arithmetic, algebra, and geometry; five years of history and the Soviet constitution; four years of geography; one year of nature study; four years of biology; three years of chemistry; two years of mechanical drawing; and four years of foreign language. Children also receive training in physical culture and fine arts. Finally, there are labor courses for the full eight years. These courses are designed to give the children a healthy respect for agricultural and industrial labor.

According to the Russians there should be no child, except in the case of brain damage or other serious illness, who cannot complete this curriculum by the time he is fifteen years of age. For those who fail (about 3 per cent) causes other than mental deficiency must be found. Children are approached on the assumption that they have capacities and develop abilities that are not measurable by intelligence quotient tests. Needless to say, I.Q. tests and similar devices are not used in the Soviet Union. Presumably, if a child fails in school, it is because of factors beyond his control, such as poor health, genetic mental damage, poor home environment, emotional imbalance, or poor teaching.

In American public schools decisions on children's intelligence and abilities are made early in the child's career. In fact, in many schools the first separation of children into so-called ability groups occurs within a few weeks after the start of the first grade. Indeed, in some of the most "modern" schools homogeneous grouping based upon supposed ability is practiced in kindergarten. In the first grade it is almost universal practice in American schools to divide the children into reading groups, classified as fast and slow, or fast, average, and slow. By the second or third grades the children in a majority of American schools have begun to take I.Q. and achievement tests for purposes of further classification. By the fourth and fifth grades in these schools the classes are often completely organized on ability group bases. Children who score highest in the various standardized tests are placed in the "fast," "bright," "honors," "advanced," "accelerated," or "gifted" classes. Children who score lowest are placed in the "slow," "dull," "retarded," or "remedial" classes.

By the time the children reach junior high school the differentiation in curriculum goes into full operation. Children are assigned or counseled into particular ability groupings, once again on the basis of the accumulation of standardized test scores begun as early as the second or third grades. To be sure, though many schools include academic performance as criteria in the homogeneous grouping of the children, the use of standardized test scores still remain the paramount consideration in the cases of millions upon millions of American school children with regard to assignment in specific homogeneously grouped classes. By high school the program tracks are clearly defined. Some children are college preparatory, some commercial students, some vocational, some general or nonspecific majors.

The significant contrast between the United States and the Soviet Union, so far as separating children for reasons of providing a differentiation in curriculum, is striking. The Russians make no formal or official decisions about the abilities of children until age fourteen or fifteen. Now, armed with an accumulation of over seven years of records and observations, and with the results of subject-matter examinations at the completion of the seventh year, a decision is made as to the kind of further schooling the children are to receive.

Certainly by the time American children reach junior high school there is enough information about them to warrant realistic decisions as to their educational future. Children who cannot read in the seventh grade, at age twelve, are not apt to become successful students in junior high or high school. They are certainly not college material. On the other hand, children in the seventh grade who read and write well have an excellent chance for succeeding in solid academic school work and should be encouraged to think in terms of college. The logic of this cannot be refuted. But the manner and the method by which these children arrived at their particular level, and the entire matter of making decisions about a child's ability and intelligence when he is six or seven years old, are open to serious question. Furthermore, the need for making such decisions at so early an age raises the question of motive. Why can one modern society, the Soviet Union, defer decision-making about a child's ability and intelligence until age fifteen, and another modern society, the United States, find it necessary to start the process of separating children according to ability as early as age six or seven? What factors are at work in decision-making which allow one modern industrial society not to concern itself with probing young children's intelligence, while another similar society finds it advantageous to do so? The answer may perhaps be found by taking a close look at some of the economic aspects of Russian and American society at the middle of the twentieth century.

In the Soviet Union today there is full employment. In the United States there are approximately 3.5 million unemployed workers. Even this figure, however, is misleading. The 3.5 million unemployed includes only those who are considered potentially employable because they have worked in recent years. There are millions more who have not worked for so long that they are no longer counted in the unemployment statistics. In addition, there are many more Americans —small-farm owners, tenant farmers, and migrant or seasonal farm workers—who work only part of the year, or, if they do work all year, have only sufficient income to allow the most marginal kind of existence. Finally, there are many who are employed as unskilled laborers in work that is often seasonal. These men and women—cannery workers, construction workers, fish-industry employees, and others—can count on working only part of the year. There are, then, in American society today many Americans who are never employed, or are employed only seasonally or on a part-time basis, and whose incomes by American norms are insufficient for maintaining a minimally acceptable standard of living. Leon Keyserling[11] states that there are 34 million Americans living in poverty; 16 million of them are children.

Although comparisons between standards of living in the Soviet Union and the United States are not germane here, a momentary digression for the purpose of clarification is pertinent. It is said that some Americans who live in poverty may be living as well as some fully employed Russians. This kind of intersocietal comparison is misleading. Within Russian society there are few social and economic outcasts; the healthy are fully employed. Shortages of consumer products and decent housing are conditions common to the entire nation. As more products and housing facilities are made available, all share in the benefits. In American society the standard of living for a majority of our people is adequate, and more than adequate, but for millions of other Americans (about 18 per cent) it remains below the acceptable mini-

[11] *Progress or Poverty: The U.S. at Crossroads* (Washington, D.C.: Washington Conference on Economic Progress, 1964).

mum limit set by our society. We have, therefore, Americans who are economic outcasts because they do not share in the affluence that is common to the majority of Americans. Whereas in the Soviet Union there are few "poor," separate and apart from the main stream of Soviet life, there are in the United States nearly a fifth of our people in this category. So far have we accepted this inevitable and unalterable condition in our culture, that we have coined a whole series of words and phrases to describe those living in poverty. We call them wetbacks, Mexes, Oakies, Arkies, white trash, niggers, cotton pickers, pick-and-shovel men, ditch diggers, hillbillies, moonshiners, bottle Indians, and so on.

Our limited employment opportunities are in evidence elsewhere, as well. In the United States today our medical schools rigidly restrict the number of students to be admitted; our law schools, schools of architecture, and other professional training institutions also reject many more applicants than they accept. This limiting of new entrants into the professions is not for lack of training facilities, as might be the case in some other countries, but is based upon a deliberate effort to limit the numbers of new professional people. Whatever the reasons, it is common knowledge that this situation obtains. In American society today we apparently do not want higher percentages than we already have of professionally trained people.

In the Soviet Union today there is need for scientifically and professionally trained people. If Russia is to surpass the United States in standard of living, it needs a much higher percentage of engineers, scientists, doctors, technicians, and so on, from among its total population. The Soviet Union is far behind us in production of consumer goods. Our affluent people have a much higher standard of living. It is essential for the Soviet Union, if it is to convince the world of the value of socialism, that it strive mightily to catch us and pass us in this century if possible. Backwardness in any form, economic or social, is a deterrent to convincing the world of the need for socialism; therefore all signs of backwardness must be removed as quickly as possible. To fulfill this need, Soviet society cannot afford to lose any potential professional man or woman. Each such loss is a failure to meet the seemingly inexhaustible demand for highly trained people.

In American society there is unemployment, seasonal employment, and semi-employment. There is no apparent pressing need for greater numbers of professional and technical personnel. Although by far the wealthiest society on earth, we accept poverty and unemployment as a fixed condition of life. (Even though Congress has recently enacted legislation calling for an antipoverty crusade, the amount of money appropriated would scarcely be enough to do away with the poverty in the state of Arizona alone, much less in the rest of the country.)

These basic differences between American and Russian society are reflected in the underlying premises upon which each has structured its public schools. Soviet society needs every man or woman who can qualify for professional or technical work. It needs no devices to eliminate children from competing in adulthood for available social and economic status positions. There is no need to choose a selective group of citizens who will have the good fortune to finish school and to obtain prestige jobs. The Soviet Union can sit back and let the children speak for themselves.

If every American child developed his potential talent, there would not be enough status jobs to absorb the number subsequently emerging as candidates for them. A way, therefore, has been found to eliminate large numbers of our children from qualifying for, and competing in the prestige job market. The Russians wait until children are fourteen or fifteen before deciding in what kinds of capacities they will best function when adults. In our society we start to make this decision as early as age six, and by the time a child is ten or eleven, his future is almost certain. If he comes from an affluent family—a family with sufficient income to provide the basic necessities of life (including a family of the lower-middle class and the fully employed "working" class)—he will be an executive, professional, semiprofessional, or skilled technician or worker; or a member of the business community unless there is some deficiency in his personality (alcoholism, etc.) which prevents him from functioning as it has been expected he would. But if the child comes from an impoverished family, he will in all probability be an unskilled worker, a migrant farmer, a member of the unemployed—an economically deprived citizen. We have developed tools with which to insure that this will happen in American society. We call them I.Q. tests, reading-readiness programs, ability groupings, etc. Our society absorbs into its professional and technical disciplines chiefly those who stem from the affluent in our culture. Economic success of parent virtually assures success of child. Economic failure of parent virtually assures economic failure of child. Our schools, answering the needs of our society, have responded to the demands for maintaining the *status quo.*

TWO

I.Q. tests and "innate" intelligence: their use in the public schools

An I.Q. examination purports to measure native intelligence. Many American educators and psychologists maintain that this test device provides information on the inherent capacities of a child and therefore are indications of how he will fare in his academic school work. These tests are structured by experts in the fields of testing, psychology, and psychometry, and are mass-produced by companies who specialize in providing schools with tools for measuring intelligence. There are two basic kinds of I.Q. tests: the first is a group test, the second an individual examination administered by a trained tester.

For obvious financial reasons the group I.Q. tests are those used by the overwhelming majority of American schools.

The group tests may last from one-half hour to two or three hours, depending upon whether a short or long form is administered. I.Q. tests consist of a series of questions and/or problems which presumably measure the ability of the child to interpret information in a particular way, or to relate something to something else. Supposedly no question is used if the answer requires specific informational knowledge. In this way it is hoped that the score achieved by a child will measure innate ability, and not learned information.

There are time limits allowed for the completion of I.Q. tests. Averages based on the scores of hundreds of thousands of children of various ages have been recorded. Norms for each age group have been established. Children who score extremely high may be classified as potential geniuses; children who score high are referred to as bright or gifted; children in the medium range are considered normal or average; children who score low are slow or dull; children who score extremely low may be classified as uneducable. Score figures may vary, depending upon which particular examination is used. The results and appraisals, however, are all based upon a standard deviation curve, established as the result of the huge number of results for each age group available to the test interpreters.

It would be futile to argue that I.Q. tests do not measure something. Every examination measures something. Whether the I.Q. test measures native intelligence, however, is another question. Those who devise the I.Q. tests and those who use them would have us believe that what a child has learned does not affect his score, since the nature of the questions is such that specific learning is not required for correct answers.

Study after study reveals that middle-class Caucasian American children do far better on I.Q. tests than do Americans who are Negro, Puerto Rican, Mexican, Indian, Filipino, or members of other minority groups. Other studies indicate that middle-class Caucasians achieve higher I.Q. scores than

Caucasians from economically deprived families. If one accepted the fact that I.Q. tests measure native intelligence, then it would logically follow that American middle-class Caucasian children have more innate intelligence than the members of American minority groups or Caucasian poverty families.

Scientific evidence from anthropology, psychology, biology, and genetics indicates that such an assumption is nonscientific and indefensible. Rare is the member of any of these professions who would even consider the possibility of innate superiority of one ethnic group over another. How, then, can we account for the superior I.Q. test scores achieved by middle-class Caucasian students? Let us look at this question of innate differences in intelligence among people of different races, and examine some of the writings of distinguished scientists concerning the value of I.Q. tests as measures of these differences.

In 1958 Dr. Audrey Shuey, a psychologist at Randolph Macon College, published a volume entitled *The Testing of Negro Intelligence*. Here, and in some subsequent works by others, the claim has been made that I.Q. test scores indicate that Negroes are less intelligent than whites and that mental inferiority can be racial in origin. This claim was made on the basis of the accumulation of hundreds of studies showing that Negroes score lower on I.Q. tests than Caucasians do.

In 1963 Melvin M. Tumin[1] of Princeton University challenged the validity of this claim. He called upon four leading American scientists to comment upon the position held by Dr. Shuey and others. These men were Dr. Henry C. Dyer, Vice-President of the Educational Testing Service, Princeton, New Jersey; Professor Silvan S. Tomkins, professor

[1] *Race and Intelligence* (New York: Anti-Defamation League, 1963).

of psychology, Princeton University; Professor Ralph H. Turner, Chairman of the Department of Sociology, University of California, Los Angeles; and Professor Sherwood L. Washburn, Chairman of the Department of Anthropology, University of California, Berkeley. The following are quotes taken directly from the statements of each of these men to questions posed by Mr. Tumin.

The first question: "In your judgment is there sufficient evidence in the Shuey volume to justify Dr. Shuey's conclusion regarding the presence of native differences between Negroes and whites and thus to reject in part or *in toto* the validity of the position taken by the social scientists in Paris?" (This refers to a UNESCO-sponsored meeting in Paris of world leaders in sociology, anthropology, psychology and genetics for the purpose of discussing superiority in intelligence of one race over another. A joint statement issued at the Paris conference stated in part:

> Whatever classification the anthropologist makes of man, he never includes mental characteristics as part of those classifications. It is now generally recognized that intelligence tests do not themselves enable us to differentiate safely between what is due to innate capacity and what is the result of environmental influences, training and education. Wherever it has been possible to make all allowances for differences in environmental opportunities, the tests have shown essential similarity in mental characteristics among all human groups. In short, given similar degrees of cultural opportunity to realize their potentialities, the average achievement of the members of each ethnic group is about the same.)

> DR. DYER: There is not sufficient evidence in the Shuey volume to justify the conclusion that there are native differences between the intelligence of whites and Negroes. As a matter of fact, the nature of intelligence tests is such that they are incapable of identifying native differences between any two groups, if indeed such genetic differences exist.

PROFESSOR TOMKINS: Dr. Shuey's conclusions that there are significant differences in the innate capacities of Negroes and whites is not supported by sufficient evidence to invalidate the position taken by the social scientists in Paris, that given similarity of cultural opportunities to realize their potentialities, the average achievement of the members of each ethnic group is about the same.

PROFESSOR TURNER: It has long been known that Negroes and whites in the United States differ on the average, but with sizeable overlap, in their performance on psychological tests of personality. But even the most avid defender of intelligence tests today will acknowledge that the tests measure the effects of opportunity to learn the kinds of items included in the tests, motivation, and meaningfulness of the items to the test-takers as well as innate capacity. Since everything we know about the Negro's status in western society leads us to believe that he is disadvantaged in all these respects in comparison with whites in otherwise similar environments, there is no reason to suppose that the relatively small average differences reflect innate intelligence. When efforts of various sorts are made to equate environments of Negro and white subjects more fully, differences in average I.Q. are lessened, as the environmental interpretation leads us to expect. Shuey acknowledges this much, but depends on two devices in reaching her conclusion. First, in her summaries she lumps together indiscriminately those studies incorporating serious efforts to control environment and those containing no such effort. Thus, she reasons that if one research study with a fatal defect in design does not prove the point, several studies all containing the same design error should be convincing. This is like saying that if I weigh myself on a scale that I know to be consistently in error, I can be confident if I weigh myself several times on the same scale and get the same results. Second, she takes as conclusive the residue of difference in I.Q. which remains after serious efforts at correction have been made. However, the corrections which have been employed are quite crude and approximate, so that there is every reason to believe that in the best of studies only part of the difference in opportunity, motivation, and meaningfulness has been controlled. Under these circumstances the reasonable interpretation is that complete control would reduce the differences between racial averages even further, to the point that they are either trivial or nonexistent.

All of the foregoing was known to the signers of the Paris statements, and no new developments since that time have supplied any basis for altered interpretation.

PROFESSOR WASHBURN: No, there is not sufficient evidence in the Shuey volume for Dr. Shuey's conclusions. Both the UNESCO statement and Dr. Shuey's are vague. The quoted statement says "about the same." Shuey says "Some native differences. . . ."

The issue is not whether there may, or may not be, some differences, but whether there are differences of an order so great that they must be considered in the operation of democratic society. Here *all* the evidence is unequivocally no.

The second question: "Are there in your judgment any satisfactory tests of native, i.e., innate or inborn intelligence? To what extent have the tests been able to free themselves of culturally specific factors, and thus become culture free?"

DR. DYER: There are no tests of native intelligence. In fact the concept of "native intelligence" is essentially meaningless. Every response to the stimulus material in intelligence tests is of necessity a *learned* response. . . .

PROFESSOR TOMKINS: There are no completely satisfactory tests of native intelligence in my opinion, nor are there ways of getting reliable estimates of native intelligence other than those now in use.

PROFESSOR WASHBURN: No. Intelligence is the interaction of nature (what is inherited) with the environment. There is no more reason to expect a culture-free intelligence than a diet-free stature. Although inheritance is important in determining stature, no one would think of comparing the stature of a well-fed and a starved group and claiming that the difference is all genetic.

The third question: "What do the standard intelligence tests test? Are we able, from the results of such tests, to make any valid inferences about native capacities? Under what conditions? Have these been observed in the volumes in front of you?"

DR. DYER: (a) What do the standard intelligence tests test? They test how well an individual has learned to perform tasks like those on the test. Most such tasks are similar to those required of the student in school. Consequently, most of the standard intelligence tests test how well the individual is likely to do in school.

(b) Are we able, from the results of such tests, to make any valid inferences about native capacities? Obviously not. You cannot make inferences about something that is meaningless.

PROFESSOR TOMKINS: The standard intelligence tests test achievements, which permits an inference of intelligence to the extent to which the following conditions have been met: (1) all subjects have had the same motivation to learn what is being tested; (2) all subjects are highly motivated to learn what is being tested; (3) all subjects have had the same practice on what is being tested; (4) all subjects have had sufficient practice so that the skill being tested is over-learned so that extrapolation for insufficient practice is not required and so that all can be compared with respect to the same ceiling of ability; (5) all subjects have had standardized guidance so that one can compare performances independent of differential advantages, and be sure that it is the same skill which is being tested; (6) all subjects have been exposed to the same amount of guidance as well as the same kind of guidance. . . .

PROFESSOR TURNER: Intelligence tests measure performance on a narrowly selected range of tasks, particularly of the sort that are involved in formal schooling as it is carried out in the United States. Inferences about native capacity depend upon assurance that opportunity, motivation, and meaningfulness are identical for all test-takers and have been identical during the period of learning the tasks which are included in the test. When I.Q. difference between subjects is quite large and environment has been similar, the scientist might possibly (but not with certainty) interpret his finding as showing some difference in native intelligence. When either differences are small or opportunities, motivation, and meaningfulness have clearly been unequal, no inference about native intelligence should be made.

PROFESSOR WASHBURN: Others can answer this much better than I. It is primarily word and number ability and speed.

All of these men agree on two major points: first, that there is no evidence to indicate that any one ethnic or racial group is more intelligent than any other, and that differences in performance on intelligence tests have no bearing on innate intelligence, but have to do only with learned responses; second, that intelligence tests do not measure innate or inborn abilities.

There are many other studies and reports available dealing with the question of I.Q. tests as measures of inborn intelligence. Some of the more pertinent are:

D. P. Ausubel [2] concluded that present intelligence tests do measure "functional or operating capacity at a given point of development" rather than innate potential, and are fair in this respect. They are unfair to the culturally deprived in that these children have fewer test-taking skills, are less responsive to speed pressure, less highly motivated, and less familiar with specific vocabulary.

J. H. Boger reported that rural children, after a five-month training period in following directions, noting details, perceiving spatial relationships, detecting likeness and difference in pictorial and geometric patterns, and developing increased coordination of eye and hand movements, made significant

---

[2] Conference on the Teaching of the Culturally Deprived Child (Buffalo, 1963).

gains in I.Q. scores. On the California test of mental maturity, for example, rural Negro children in grades one through four gained an average of 15.2 points over previous scores on the same test, while rural whites in the same group gained an average of 14.9 points. He concluded:

> The extent of improvement as a result of training indicates (1) that scores from I.Q. tests often give an estimate of mental ability which is an injustice to these pupils so far as actual ability is concerned, and (2) that perpetual training remedies some of the handicaps which influence performance of rural children on group I.Q. tests. It would appear that rural elementary school children are capable of responding to a more challenging school program than I.Q. scores derived from group intelligence tests frequently seem to justify.[3]

A. D. B. and A. M. Clarke reported that among a group of mentally retarded they studied, I.Q. scores showed significant increase after the environment of the subjects was improved. They observed:

> It is consistent with this finding to suggest that the environment which is really antagonistic towards the child retards mental development for many years. Later, however, after removal from such conditions this retardation begins to fade, and I.Q. increments occur, often at ages when mental growth is commonly assumed to have ceased.[4]

K. Eells stated:

> . . . most presently used intelligence tests . . . are so constructed and so administered that scores on them are influenced by the cultural backgrounds of the children taking the test in such a way that children from certain kinds of

---

[3] "An Experimental Study of the Effects of Perceptual Training on Group I.Q. Scores of Elementary Pupils in Rural Ungraded Schools," *Journal of Educational Research*, XLVI (1952), 43-53.
[4] "How Constant is the I.Q.?," *Lancet*, II (1953), 877-80.

backgrounds receive scores that are not accurate reflections of their basic intelligence.[5]

T. Pettigrew[6] wrote that the severely deprived environment of the average Negro child can lower his measured I.Q. in two ways: first, it can act to deter his actual intellectual development by presenting him with such a constricted encounter with the world that his innate potential is barely tapped; and second, it can act to mask his actual functioning intelligence in the test situation by not preparing him culturally and motivationally for such a middle-class task.

W. F. Brazziel and Mary Terrell [7] reported on a study made of 26 first-grade Negro children. After a six-week readiness program, including parent meetings once a week, thirty minutes of educational TV watched in the home, and a readiness program to develop vocabulary, perception, word reasoning, and ability to follow directions, the following results were obtained: the group reached the 50th percentile on readiness as measured by the Metropolitan Readiness Test, while three nonexperimental classes in the same school were at the 15th percentile. The I.Q. median for the control group was 106.5, whereas the general expectation for this age group in this school was 90.

In light of the foregoing remarks regarding I.Q. tests and their value as predictors of intelligence, it is difficult to imagine that the overwhelming majority of public school districts in the United States have relied upon I.Q. tests for many

[5] "Some Implications for School Practice of the Chicago Studies of Cultural Bias in Intelligence Tests," *Harvard Educational Review*, XXIII (1953), 284-97.

[6] "Negro American Intelligence: A New Look at an Old Controversy," *Journal of Negro Education*, XXXIII (1964), 6-25.

[7] "An Experiment in the Development of Readiness in a Culturally Disadvantaged Group of First Grade Children," *Journal of Negro Education*, XXXI (1962), 4-7.

years as means for determining the innate intelligence of children. It is just as shocking to realize that great numbers of public school districts have used I.Q. test scores as one of the most important devices for grouping children according to their supposed inborn ability. It must be emphasized again that this practice is so common in American public schools as to be considered an integral part of the policy and procedure of the institution of public education. Indicative of the importance of I.Q. tests in the behavior of American school districts are the findings of a study by Victor B. Elkin, Janet Kulberg, and James A. Miller[8] encompassing 85 per cent of the school districts in Long Island, New York. The study showed that all but one of these school districts use group I.Q. tests. Eighty-five per cent of the districts reporting put the results of group I.Q. testing to immediate use for counseling, screening, grouping, and other purposes. The other 15 per cent used the results in indirect ways.

The literature concerning American education and psychology abounds with examples of the significant place I.Q. testing, results, and interpretation have had in the treatment of children by the public school. The research cited is typical of the findings made by researchers concerned with this type of study. A great deal of comment appeared in newspapers and magazines after the decision of the New York City Board of Education to do away with I.Q. tests as a means of diagnosing the potential ability of children. The reasons offered by the School Board were that these tests are unfair to minority-group children and are not true measures of innate intelligence. However, rather than discarding the notion that inborn intelligence can and should be measured, New York City schools have entered into "an experimental effort

[8] "Survey of Group I.Q. Practices," *Journal of Educational Research*, LVII (1964), 105.

to develop valid culture-fair measuring techniques of learning potential." [9] Thus, they are still concerned with finding out as quickly as possible how "intelligent" the children are; they just don't like the present measuring devices.

Since the middle-class Caucasian children do much better in I.Q. tests than other children, it inevitably follows that in great numbers of American public schools the affluent Caucasian children are placed in the fast academic classes, while a majority of the other children are adjudged academically slower and assigned to the less academically oriented classes. Again the question arises, why do we rely upon devices of such questionable validity as I.Q. tests to segregate our children? It is apparently because the use of I.Q. scores so aptly meets the requirements of present American society with regard to providing, through education, the kinds of opportunities we wish to have available for children of the two different economic backgrounds.

[9] *Phi Delta Kappan,* XLVI (1964), 105.

THREE

Formal and informal
techniques of alienation

It is taken for granted everywhere in our country that reading and writing skills are the keys that open the doors to jobs of prestige. Since today college training is almost synonymous with entrance into the prestigious professional, semi-professional, executive, and semi-executive world, the ability to read and write well becomes a basic requirement for success. Millions of Americans are functionally illiterate; they cannot read or write well enough to be able to use these skills as part of their everyday work. Whitney Young of the Urban League states that 70 per cent of Americans who come from minority groups are below minimum literacy expectancy for employment in jobs of prestige. The Council for Basic Education maintains that nearly 40 per cent of all Americans are functionally illiterate.

What these percentages mean, or how accurate they

are, is not really the issue. What is important is that educators in America are aware that millions of American school children cannot read, or at best, are reading at levels well below their age expectancy. More remarkable is the fact that educators apparently have come to accept this condition as inevitable and have done little to introduce significant new practices to overcome this pattern of illiteracy and semiliteracy. It is true that many remedial programs, reading clinics, and so on, have appeared in recent years, but these are for the most part inadequate for dealing with the depth of the problem. There is little research in evidence to show that we are producing fewer functional illiterates today than ten years ago. Although controversy has raged around the various methods of teaching reading, such as phonics versus sight, there are few signs that all of this interest has resulted in impressive advances toward eradicating illiteracy or semiliteracy. Despite all of the uproar in the last decade about why and what Johnny can't read, it appears that millions of Johnnies still cannot read. Even if we do not in theory accept reading failures as inevitable, we act as if we do, and this is just as indefensible.

It is common practice in the early elementary grades to divide children into reading groups, based on supposed ability or reading readiness. These groups are rarely called fast, medium, or slow; usually they have other designations. They may be called the Robin, Blue Bird, or Sparrow groups; or the Buffalo, Deer, and Elk groups. The purpose of such meaningless terms is to deceive the children. It is theorized that it is harmful to tell a child that he is in a slow group. However, few children are so stupid as to be fooled by this subterfuge. They know which group they are in because they know they are being grouped, and one needs only eyesight to figure out which groups have the more difficult or advanced books. What is interesting is that we recognize the need for attempting to show the children that none of them has been designated as fast, medium, or slow. We feel, and rightly so, that being stigmatized as a slow reader may have a damaging psychological effect upon a child. Feelings of inadequacy are not conducive to best effort among most children. However, though we may recognize the practice as questionable, we do not seem to be willing to do something to correct it.

If it were possible to show that the purpose of reading groups was to identify the weakest readers so that a great deal more time and effort could be spent working with them, then some justification for this practice might be found. More often than not, just the opposite is true. The children in the slower reading groups are assumed to be academically un-talented and the level of expectancy for them is greatly lowered. Instead of spending more time with them, the teacher spends less, reasoning that time spent with the non-academic is a waste. It is a logical assumption that if a child shows little reading ability, he will not do very well scholas-tically. Why, therefore, put one's available energy into work-ing with children who cannot profit from the experience when, indeed, they may suffer traumatic shock because they have been asked to go beyond their capacities? Jules Henry, writing of a third-grade classroom he observed, states:

> Now Group II, the poorer readers, occupy the seats deserted by Group I. Teacher seems very tired now, and goes through the lesson mechanically. Her voice is weak and she leans against the blackboard.[1]

This, after Henry has described the great amount of enthusi-asm of the teacher in working for nearly forty minutes with Group I.

[1] "Spontaneity, Initiative, and Creativity in Suburban Class-rooms," *Journal of Orthopsychiatry*, XXIX (1959), 266-79.

As time goes on the children of the slower groups get further and further behind the children of the fast. The rationale for this phenomenon is twofold: (1) the children in the slow groups are incapable of doing what the children of the fast groups can do, so why burden them with what they cannot achieve? (2) the less that is offered, the poorer becomes their reading in comparison with the other children, until the time comes when their reading levels are so far behind the levels of the fast that they truly can no longer expect to compete with them.

Obviously, if children in the first grade are to be grouped according to reading ability, some criterion must be used. I.Q. tests cannot be employed because the reading level of children in the first grade is not sufficiently high. Teachers therefore must rely upon other techniques in making their selections for the reading groups. Some children can read and write their names when they enter the first grade; some even know the alphabet and can spell the names of a half-dozen of their favorite baseball players or movie stars. Some children cannot read or write anything and do not know A from B. Lacking any other kind of indication, a teacher must rely upon observation of these varying degrees of ability so as to assign her children to particular groups. One group is clearly ready and sails into reading at full speed. One group is apparently not ready and will spend a long time before it even can get started.

We know that children who have pencils, books, magazines, paper, scrabble sets, and so on, at home, are much more apt to be "ready" to read when they begin school. We know that children who come from homes where reading is emphasized, where praise is given for precociousness, and where a whole expectancy for reading and writing is in evidence, are much more liable to be ready when they get to first grade. On the other hand, we know that children who come from homes where books, magazines, paper, and pencils are almost nonexistent, and where praise for academic talent is not part of pre-school life, very likely will not be ready when they reach the first grade. Thus, some children come prepared for school; others do not. Those who are prepared are adjudged able, and in the greatest number of cases they learn to read with little difficulty. Many of those who are not prepared are adjudged less able or "unready" to learn to read, and are treated accordingly. They are sheltered from any but the most minimal exposure to reading, and as a result they often scarcely learn to read at all. Determination as to children's abilities are made not on the basis of what they could be, but on the basis of what they are in October of their first year of school.

It is argued by some that these groups are not rigid in the sense that once in, never out—that they are to make children feel comfortable and that when change, particularly upward, is called for, change will be made. This view is very difficult to support. How does one compete with others who have all of the advantages? How does a child, who is expected by the teacher not to perform well, change the teacher's opinion when she controls the devices and techniques that insure that the child will not perform well? How does a child who is reading only three- and four-letter words hope to emerge out of his group to join the group of children who at the same time have begun to read three-syllable words? Grouping on the basis of reading ability in the first grade precipitates the academic success, or lack of it, for millions of American children.

We know through observation and research studies that literacy in such European countries as Switzerland, Germany, Denmark, and Finland is much higher than ours. Assuredly no one would suggest that children of these countries are brighter than American children, or that it is significantly easier to learn to read Danish or Finnish than it is to learn English. Illiteracy or semiliteracy need not be. These are culture traits, and if they exist in high percentage in a particular society, the real reasons must be sought out. Children who are healthy, physically and emotionally, who do not learn to read must lack motivation to do so. Few children fail to learn to read due to lack of intelligence or ability. The vast majority of American children of affluent families learn to read. The majority of Negro, Mexican, Puerto Rican, Indian, and economically deprived white children do not learn to read and write well. Why? Surely the answer must be cultural rather than biological. Why is there less motivation to learn to read among the children of the economically deprived? Is it because these children have poor teaching? If so, why? Is it because they do not care about learning to read? If so, why? Is it because they see no reason for learning to read? If so, why? What circumstances in American society cause many of these children to find no value in learning to read effectively? What are the conditions that cause great numbers of them to become the recipients of poor and uninspired teaching in the area of reading?

American children by the millions do not learn to read effectively because American society has given them no reason for expanding the effort toward gaining something which, to them, has little value. If they learned to read effectively, a serious dislocation in our economic structure could ensue. So long as millions of Americans are functionally illiterate there is no need to absorb them into the main stream of American life, to compete for status jobs. In a society where the numbers of professional, semiprofessional, executive, and semi-executive personnel are limited, it would be folly and even hazardous to encourage the millions of children of the economically deprived to enter the competitive arena. It is not suggested that we do not need more professionally trained people in a service sense, only that those who control these professions, such as the American Medical Association, rigidly restrict the numbers allowed to enter into training. As yet American society has not shown sufficient concern about the shortage of medical personnel in many parts of our country to bring enough pressure upon the AMA to vastly increase opportunities for medical training. Without this pressure, we can only assume that the professional groups like the AMA, the American Dental Association, the American Bar Association, and the professional architects' and certified public accountants' organizations will continue to call the tune. For obvious reasons shortage of personnel is advantageous to those already in these professions.

It is not only the professional organizations in America that limit opportunity for those who wish to enter into particular occupations. Many of our craft unions have been virtually closed enterprises for a long time. In many American cities the only way to become a union carpenter, electrician, plumber, mason, bricklayer, and so on is to have a father, uncle, or close friend who is a member of the union and thus able to secure an apprenticeship for you. Since few if any of the economically deprived have such access, the consequences of this policy are all too evident. In San Francisco, until very recently only one or two of the craft unions had any Negro membership and those that did exhibited the grossest kind of tokenism.

One does not need to read in order to pick fruit, tear up railroad track, exist on a reservation, labor as a tenant farmer, work a three-acre farm in the Ozarks, be a sharecropper, make whisky in the Tennessee mountains, push a broom, or tear open a monthly relief check. These are the tasks which few American men and women of the affluent class would seriously consider worthy occupations, but they are the occupations to which millions of the economically deprived are relegated. Great numbers of the economically deprived do not need to learn to read, and they do not.

There is nothing inherent or God-given in wanting to learn to read. One does so because one sees reason for reading or is expected to learn to read. Most six-year-old children, of course, do not say, if I learn to read I'll get good grades, and good grades will get me into the college prep program, and the college prep program will get me into college, and college will get me a good job or a good husband. But some six-year-old children do know how important it is to learn to read because they understand that they need to do so if they are to *belong*. Others accept learning to read as a natural step along the path that leads to growing up. Father and Mother read, brothers and sisters read, older friends read and talk about it; the whole world reads. Father and Mother have talked about reading, have encouraged him to learn the letters and spell his name, and have played games with him involving letters, words, rhymes, and spelling. Everyone in his world expects him to read, and he assumes that reading is as natural as speaking. For him, it is as easy to learn to read correctly as it is to learn to speak correctly. In a world where reading is school in the first grade, and school is reading in the first grade, there is almost no chance that a healthy child will fail to learn to read unless unexpected factors intervene.

In some six-year-olds' homes, however, things are quite different. Father and Mother do not read, except perhaps a few simple necessary things; brothers and sisters do not read; older friends don't have time to read or have never learned to read. Father and Mother may tell him to do well in school, but words do not make up his world, they merely confuse it. The concept of reading as a natural part of growing up is beyond his understanding. The millions of children from such environments rarely learn to read beyond a third- or fourth-grade level. This is not to say that some of the children of the economically deprived do not learn to read, and read well; but there are more that do not learn to read well than do.

What is it that creates such an atmosphere? As has been pointed out, reading is of little importance to nearly 20 per cent of our population. School is the same. School not only tries to teach him unimportant things, but attempts to make him something he is not, and doesn't want to be. School is for those who can suffer through it; school is for the "other" kids, kids not of his world. Reading means school, and school means reading, so why bother?

Hence, lack of motivation is a significant element in explaining why millions of American children do not learn to read. This is not to say that because one belongs to the economically deprived it automatically follows that he will not learn to read. What is true is that whereas few children of affluent parents are insufficiently motivated to learn to read, millions of the economically deprived are.

Lack of motivation, however, is not the entire answer to the disgrace of American illiteracy. Good teachers can motivate. Respected and admired teachers, who in turn have respect for, and faith in, children's ability, and who transmit this feeling to the children, can bring about miracles even when motivation may be initially lacking. Unfortunately, this kind of teacher is hard to find in schools with large numbers of economically deprived children. Just as unfortunately, particularly in the southern part of the United States, teachers of economically deprived children—many of whom desire to do a good job—frequently lack the kind of preparation needed to be a successful teacher of reading and other academic curricula.

In the South today, many teachers in schools where there are large numbers of economically deprived children are only high school graduates or, at best, have had one or two years of "normal school" teacher training. These teachers often were themselves graduated from schools where their teachers were only high school graduates or had a minimum of college training. Concern, desire, and willingness to do good work comes to little if knowledge and understanding are lacking. Arthur L. Benson, Director of the Teaching Program for the Educational Testing Service, has said:

> Unless the vicious circle is broken, whereby large numbers of undereducated American teachers are permitted to undereducate other generations of Americans, it is futile to hope that the gap between an adequate schooling for large numbers of children, and quality education for others, will be closed in Southern education.[2]

The fact of lower salaries for teachers in the South also contributes to the difficulties in attracting knowledgeable teachers into the public schools. In Arkansas, for example, the average salary for a teacher is about $4,000 a year; beginning salaries start as low as $2,400 a year; in Louisiana, Alabama, Mississippi, South Carolina, West Virginia, Georgia, and Tennessee salaries are often scarcely higher than in Arkansas. In Mississippi the average salary for a teacher is $4,150 a year. Compare these salaries with those in California, New York, Connecticut, and other northern industrial states. In California the state minimum is $5,000 a year for beginning teachers and the average yearly salary is just under $8,000 (nearly double that of Arkansas or Mississippi), and in some northern districts maximum salaries exceed $10,000. Low salaries attract poorly trained teachers, cause poor morale, lead to attrition and an "I don't give a damn" attitude. Indifference and poor teaching, whatever their causes, are not

---

[2] "Ten Years of Deliberate Speed," *American Education* (Washington, D.C.: U.S. Department of Health, Education, and Welfare), January 1965, pp. 1-3.

what is needed for the children of the economically deprived.

In the North poor teaching of the economically deprived can often be traced to causes other than inadequate training and low salaries. To be sure, nowhere are good teachers paid as well as they should be; however, in most northern areas where economically deprived children are found, salaries are sufficient to maintain a fairly decent standard of living. Low morale and negativism in these northern schools grow from different roots. Among the basic reasons are: (1) the inability of affluent-society-oriented teachers to understand the behavior of these children, particularly those from ethnic minority groups; (2) the tendency on the part of the more able teachers to seek schools where there are "nicer" and "more educable" children; able teachers have no difficulty in finding a place in other schools, poorly regarded teachers who seek transfer often find it hard to shift because other schools do not want them; (3) the lack of adequate facilities in many schools with large numbers of economically deprived children: since these children, particularly those from minority groups, usually live in the older parts of our northern cities, the schools generally are the oldest and most poorly equipped in the school district. Affluent whites today live in the newer areas of the cities or in the great sprawling suburbs that have developed since the end of World War II. Here the schools are newer, the equipment more modern, and the facilities more up-to-date.

All human beings bring their value commitments to their relationships with others. How one perceives another is often determined by one's own values and behavior. The teacher is no exception. How she views the child may have a serious effect upon how this child feels toward his school. If a teacher does not understand the specific kinds of behavior of certain children, she will make this feeling known to the child, even though she may not intend to. The inability of affluent-oriented teachers in American society to understand or cope with the behavior of children from economically deprived families is often of paramount importance in alienating these children from the public schools. It is this clash of value commitments that, more than any other factor, drives our Negro, Mexican, Puerto Rican, Indian, and economically deprived Caucasian children out of the school and into the street. Children abandon school in the second grade attitudinally, and in the tenth physically, not because they are "stupid" but because they don't care. They have been estranged from school; they have been attacked at the point of greatest vulnerability, their own value structure. This alienation process is as common in the South as it is in the North; it is interwoven into the fabric of our public school system.

Teachers are guardians and disseminators of the existing mores. Our moral precepts and practices are made an integral part of the curriculum process in our public schools. Jules Henry states, "The prime effort of the adult world is *to make child attitudes look organized to adults.*" [3]

Most important to the teacher are indications from her students that their behavior is being organized in such a way that the following results emerge: (1) the children use "decent" language as opposed to vulgar or obscene language; (2) the children employ grammatically correct language; (3) the children exhibit "clean" attitudes toward sex and drinking; (4) the children believe in talking over one's problems rather than fighting about them; (5) the children exhibit an understanding of the relationship between effort and reward as being important to future success.

[3] "Attitude Organization in Elementary Classrooms," *American Journal of Orthopsychiatry*, XXVII (1957), 117-33.

Some children find it difficult to convince the teacher that they are being properly indoctrinated. These children will suffer as a result. They will find it hard, indeed, to gain the teacher's approval. Without this approval school becomes a dreaded experience and identity with school is easily shattered. School and child early reach a parting of the ways.

This is not to say that *all* elementary school teachers are preoccupied only with morality lessons. However, the institution of the public school as an instrument of dominant American culture is dedicated to maintaining the prevailing behavior patterns of that culture. Students are fortunate now and again to have a teacher in elementary school whose concerns are with matters other than an *a priori* defense of these beliefs. She may be committed to them, but does not find it necessary to attack children who are not. The overwhelming majority of children in American public schools will at some time be exposed to teachers whose commitment to affluent-society traditions so colors her behavior as to make it impossible for her to tolerate opposition.

For the children of the affluent these traditions fit comfortably, but for many of the children of the economically deprived they are completely foreign. For the elementary teacher the dissemination of these traditions is essential to making her job worthwhile; she does not enjoy prestige or status in American society because of her ability to accumulate material goods; her self-esteem comes from the knowledge that she is making a contribution to her society by transmitting proper, "decent" standards to the children in her care. She can afford to allow little opposition to her role as surrogate of affluent-society ethics. She is responsible—to the affluent parents and to the community—for turning out children who will be "fit" for acceptance into dominant American culture.

Two points must now be considered: First, what are the

circumstances that make it obligatory for teachers in public schools to accept the assumptions on what constitutes proper behavior? Second, why do economically deprived children find it so difficult to accept these principles, and how does their eventual alienation from school come about?

To say we are creatures of our culture is to say nothing. In a society as socially and economically heterogeneous as ours, we must define culture quite carefully. What culture are we creatures of? What culture are we committed to? Particularly is it necessary to understand what is meant by "our culture" when we consider the public school.

The culture pattern to which most of our teachers are committed is diametrically opposed to the culture patterns of millions of economically deprived children. Teachers for the most part come from established, affluent homes or are committed to the values common to American dominant culture. Many of the economically deprived children come from homes where there is constant struggle to secure even the most basic necessities of life. Teachers see education as a means to future success and fulfillment. They stress the possibility of attaining prestige through academic accomplishment and book learning; they exhort children to forego temporary pleasures for future rewards. Many of the economically deprived children do not understand success and fulfillment in terms of the future. They have few models around them to confirm the validity of the proposition that school education and book learning lead to success. Many of the economically deprived children find that the greatest prestige comes from behavior thoroughly disapproved by the public school—sexual prowess, ability to fight, and development of cunning in circumventing established law. Many of these children believe only in today, because tomorrow is just another day of poverty, broken home, jail, or even worse. The teacher is given the task of convincing them that their values, commitments, indeed much of their entire lives, are wrong. A majority of these children, with remarkable strength, reject this assumption.

Is it any wonder that our public schools have failed dismally with this group of children? The failure of the public schools has been the failure of American society as a whole to show genuine concern for the plight of the economically deprived and the ethnically scorned in our nation. One need only look at Harlem, San Antonio, Navajo land, Appalachia, rural Mississippi, and ten thousand other such places, to see what has become of potentially capable human beings.

It has already been demonstrated how the use of culturally based I.Q. tests affect the school careers of untold numbers of American children, how scores achieved on these tests are a strong factor in relating to particular class sections supposedly based upon innate ability. It has been shown that the economically deprived, because of their poor initial reading performance and their lack of motivation, do poorly in such examinations, are therefore adjudged early in their lives as slow or dull students and treated accordingly. It has also been shown how the practice of dividing children into fast and slow reading groups in the first grade places the economically deprived children in academic situations involving reading in which little is expected of them and less is asked of them; an assumption that they are academically untalented is based upon appraisals of the abilities they bring with them as they first enter school, rather than on what they might be ten years later.

Again it should be stressed that grouping for reading would be justifiable if its purpose were to give greater and more substantial aid to the initially slower students. Unfortunately this is not the case, and often quite the opposite is true. These children, in the name of shielding them against the rigors of academically oriented schooling, are presented with a watered-down curriculum including a slowed-up reading course. It is further assumed by the school personnel responsible for the grouping that by removing the students who are slow at the start, the "bright," "ready" children are freed to move ahead unimpeded by the others.

Thus the formal methods of alienating children from public schools are easily identified. First, they are classified as academically untalented because they bring with them to school few of the skills needed to be appraised as potentially able. Eunice Shaed Newton writes:

> When the early environment of the child is not book-centered, is bereft of the arts, and is lacking in conversations about the happenings of the world then he is likely to enter school unmotivated, diffident, "inwardizing," unaware, and uninterested. Perceptual unreadiness is similarly a by-product of the naturally depressed community.[4]

Second, they are assigned to the slow reading groups, their curriculum is diluted, they are given I.Q. and other standardized tests in the second, third, or fourth grades, to re-enforce what had already been determined about them, and they are placed under teachers who have little understanding or patience with their patterns of behavior. All that is needed now to complete their isolation from affluent American society is to be driven away from the schools by a frontal attack upon their own systems of self-esteem and their most powerful commitments.

It may be said with little reservation that a child's commitments affect his attitudes and behavior; commitment is synonymous with subjective identity. All of us relate to our social structure in recognizable ways, otherwise we cannot be functioning members of our society. Most children have com-

[4] "The Culturally Deprived Child in Our Verbal Schools," *Journal of Negro Education*, XXXI (1962), 187.

mitment to family. It does not matter whether the family occupies a thirty-room home at Newport Beach, or a one-and-a-half-room apartment in Spanish Harlem. Commitment to family does not always signify total approval of family. It has to do more with one's roots in a particular time and space. Commitment to family is belonging to something. It is having a way of life and a pattern of behavior that is consistent, recognized, and understood. Even those children who flee from home at the earliest opportunity do not in many cases shake off their commitment to family. Indeed, as time goes on and even if separation is of long duration, the attitudes of family often survive and reappear as a strong influence. Even economically deprived children who come from broken, transient, or unstable homes bring with them to school a way of thinking and an identity with their own specific patterns of behavior. If their customs and habits are challenged by school and teacher, the children are placed in the position of having to choose between the ways of their families and a whole new set of suppositions. Almost all children of the economically deprived, especially if they attend school with children of the affluent, are faced with this choice early in their elementary school career. Either father, mother, brothers, sisters, uncles, aunts, grandparents, friends, neighbors, and their world is right, or the world of school and teachers is right. It should come as no surprise that the greater majority of these children who bring so-called unacceptable values to school, cling to them, fend off the attack, and finally deny the worth and significance of those who launch the attack.

In the formal atmosphere of the classroom, teachers representing affluent-society culture demand of the economically deprived children that they renounce the ways of their fathers and of the world they know and consider to be real. That large numbers of these children do not accede to the wishes of the teachers is indication of the power of commitment to a particular way of doing. That the consequences of their refusal are irreparably damaging to them in any attempt they might make toward joining the mainstream of American society is, of course, a tragedy.

What is the climate in our public schools that forces nearly a third of our children to the sidelines? Mention has been previously made of five unassailable assumptions that constitute a strong part of the moral backbone of American affluent society. Let us now see what effect each has upon the economically deprived child:

1. *Children should use decent language as opposed to vulgar language.*   There is a myth in American society that nice people do not swear or use obscene language. Vulgarity is a sign of poor breeding or bad manners. Like many other myths, this one receives strong support in the public schools. Four-letter Anglo-Saxon "bad" words are anathema. Even the innocuous and most universal terms in our language used by both men and women, such as *hell* and *damn*, are taboo in the classroom. There can be little argument against this position. School is not the place to encourage children to use what is described in "decent" society as the language of the streets.

Unfortunately, as might be expected, the need to defend propriety by barring vulgar language in the schools has ramifications far beyond the teacher's correction of infractions on the part of the students. Attendant upon the use of objectionable language by the children is a whole series of problems. First, it should be understood that despite the myth, vulgar language is not just the language of the streets; it is the language of all Americans. The words are spoken in the homes of people representing all social and economic strata in American society. Humor based on these words and alluding to them are as common in the Pacific Club in San Francisco and over bridge tables in Westchester County as in South Chicago's bars and pool halls. Second, despite the universality of the use of vulgar language in American society, there does exist a significant class distinction. Children of affluent parents are for the most part protected against hearing such language. Parents of these children do not, or at least are supposed not to use vulgar language in the presence of the children. Such language among the children themselves is prohibited. Jokes at an adult gathering, the themes of which are vulgar and/or obscene, are permitted; resorting to vulgar language to make a point or as an expletive to express anger or frustration may be acceptable, but only so long as children are not present.

There is, then, a clear demarcation in language use between adults and children living together in affluent society, with a consequent forbidding sort of aura around the "bad" words. Nevertheless, children in affluent society, one way or the other, learn the bad words and use them where no adult can supposedly overhear. They do this with a sort of titillating intrigue and daring. Girls are expected to express shock and to protest when boys say the prohibited words. But among themselves they may show little inhibition in employing the words. In fact, they may enjoy doing so, not because the words are part of their usual vocabulary, but precisely because they are not. Vulgar language among affluent children, then, is something to be hidden, giggled over, enjoyed, braved, shared with friends. Because this language for affluent children is for themselves alone, to be kept secret from adult ears, the children have no difficulty in avoiding the use of vulgar language in school; it can be shut off at will since it is not part of the everyday conversation.

Most children of the economically deprived have a different set of experiences with regard to language. Vulgar language is as much a part of their lives as is saying *ain't* and *it don't.* In the ghettos of our cities and in the rural areas of the South or North, wherever the black, white, or in-between economically deprived live, vulgar language is in common use all around them. Children are not sheltered from language, nor is there thought to be any reason they should be. In the home, on the stoop of a Harlem tenement where ten or fifteen Negro children are gathered, boys and girls alike, the four-letter words of Chaucer vintage will enter the conversation as casually as *the* and *and.* There is nothing secret, daring, or mysterious about such language. It is speaking. Not to use it is to speak a different language.

For these children school means a different language. They need constantly to be on guard. If they are to avoid censure they must always be aware of where they are. Of course, caution does not always operate, and slips occur. Any veteran of the Armed Forces, on coming home to his family after some years of talking in the barracks, knows how difficult it is and what a strenuous effort he must exert to clean up his language. Children of the economically deprived fight this battle in school every day. Many lose. Many more barely hold their own. Still more don't really care.

The children from the ghetto speak clearly and freely a language that is real and universal, and they suffer. The other children deceive and are rewarded. To the ghetto child the school once again becomes alien; it praises what is profoundly opposed to his real environment as something worthwhile and to be emulated. He finds shame where he would like to feel none. He suffers penalty because of spontaneity. The children of the affluent talk two languages and are praised. The children of the economically deprived speak one language and are condemned.

William Melvin Kelley states:

> The American Negro feels he can, on the spur of the moment, create the most exciting language that exists in any

English-speaking country today. I asked someone what they feel about white people trying to use "hip" language. He said: "Man, they blew the gig just by being gray." [5]

The economically deprived child in the public school has "blown the gig" just because he is what he is.

2. *Children should employ grammatically correct language.* Eunice Shaed Newton states:

> In our culture the educated person must have mastery of the standard usage of his mother tongue in order to be reasonably literate; functional literacy, moreover, is basic to even marginal participation in our way of life.[6]

The use of *ain't* or double negatives cannot be tolerated in the classroom of the public schools. So it is that from the beginning the children who use this kind of unacceptable language are supposed to be corrected by the teacher. (That some teachers do not may often be traced to their own poor language habits, most common among poorly trained teachers in some southern areas where almost all of the children attending class are economically deprived.) None can dispute the duty and right of the teacher to help children learn to speak the language correctly. How successful is the teacher in her effort is another question. No more clear-cut example of the lack of positive influence of the public schools on the economically deprived children may be seen than in determining how many actually give up their incorrect language. Can it be possible, after all those years in elementary school, that the overwhelming majority of these children continue to speak a language unacceptable to the public schools despite the constant correction by teachers? It is certainly pos-

[5] "If You're Woke, You Dig It," *The New York Times Magazine,* May 20, 1962, p. 50.
[6] Newton, *op. cit.,* p. 185.

sible, because it is true. This in itself should tell a great deal about the relationship between the economically deprived children and the public schools. Werner Cohn states:

> Difficulties caused by the differences in language probably contribute to the fairly widespread disaffection of lower class children from our public school culture.[7]

But, while little success is attained in changing language usage, a great deal is done toward alienating these children by criticizing them. For hand in hand with the effort to change language usage goes the effort to change value commitments. Whereas the teacher most often fails to do either, she succeeds in the latter case in forcing the economically deprived children to rebel against school, teachers, and the whole surrounding *milieu*. In her efforts, often sincere, to help these children overcome their handicaps, she forces them to reject school values in defense of their own. After Johnny has said for the fiftieth time, "Teacher, I ain't got no pencil," and teacher has replied, pushed beyond patience, desperate to uphold her position as surrogate of "correct" culture, "Only people who are uneducated or ignorant say 'ain't'; it's wrong," what more needs to be said? Perhaps the teacher means no harm. She has a job to do and she is doing it the best she knows how. She may be right. Maybe only uneducated and ignorant people do say *ain't*. Johnny may not even know what "ignorant" and "uneducated" mean, except that they connote something bad. He does know that his father and mother say *ain't*, and his brothers and sisters, friends and relatives say *ain't*. His real world says *ain't* (sometimes even the preacher says *ain't*). Only the teachers do not, and of course some of the "other" kids in class. No one else. No one

---

[7] "On the Language of Lower Class Children," *School Review,* LXVII (Winter 1959), 435.

in his world is one bit afraid to say *ain't*. In fact, no one ever even thinks about it. What can Johnny do now? He can accept the teacher's world and say *haven't* and try to join her in her way of speaking, or he can say *ain't* and stay with family, friends, and his way of living. She has forced him to make a choice *not because she tried to correct him,* but because she made the matter of language a basis for conflict over value commitment. She has now pushed him into the dilemma of having to reject the world that gives him his place and his security if he accepts what the teacher says, because she has denigrated the ways of those closest to him.

Does this mean that teachers should not correct Johnny? Of course not. It does mean that in helping him to become aware of correct language she must not cloud the issue by introducing extraneous and threatening elements. Teacher can say to Johnny, "Next time you start to say *ain't*, try to say *haven't* instead, because it's supposed to be a better way. When I was a little girl in the first grade, I used to say *ain't* sometimes, and so did my brothers, and it took me the longest time to change. Even now I find myself almost saying *ain't* sometimes. So next time, try to remember to say *haven't*, and if you forget, we'll see who remembers first that you forgot."

With what is known today about the lack of success teachers have in changing the language of the economically deprived, certainly this method would not produce less success. Even if little change were effected, at least the children would not be placed in the position of having to choose between value systems, and thus to reject either family or school. Indeed, one writer has gone so far as to suggest that attacks upon children's language are directly related to attacks upon their behavior and value structure. James B. McMillan states:

> There is not a single iota of objective factual evidence for saying that *are not* is more legitimately English than

ain't. Philologists can, however, find evidence that people in some social contexts punish the user of *ain't.* . . . If the language habits of one group of people are respected or disliked by other people, the respect or dislike is a matter of social psychology, not of grammar.[8]

3. *Children should exhibit "clean" attitudes toward sex, drinking, and generally loose behavior.* There is a close resemblance in this expectancy and that regarding the use of decent language. One kind of American adolescent enters into sexual and drinking activities with little concealment. Another enters into these activities at about the same age, but no one seems to know it, or at least admit they know anything about it. Sixteen-year-old Mexican boys in Los Angeles drink in the streets, or in the house, or on their porches. Sixteen-year-old boys and girls from Beverly Hills or Santa Barbara go out to the beach or up to the mountains after dark and do the same. Sixteen-year-old Negroes who live in the ghettos make love in pool halls, parks, living rooms, and anywhere else that is available. Girls from affluent society get pregnant in automobiles after dark, down lonely country roads, or at beach parties miles away from the camp fires. The children of the economically deprived, just as they do not hide their vulgar language, do not make any great effort to conceal from adults this part of their lives. The children of the affluent act out the same behavior, hide it, and give affluent American society the image it wants.

In a recent study completed in one of California's most urban and suburban counties, it was found that the highest rate of pregnancy among high school girls occurred in those schools where the students represented the most affluent families in the county. A year or so later in this same county,

---

[8] "A Philosophy of Language," in Harold B. Allen, ed., *Readings in Applied English Linguistics* (New York: Appleton-Century-Crofts, Inc., 1958), p. 205.

an entirely affluent and Caucasian community, where the average home costs in excess of $30,000, was plagued by bands of as many as fifty children aged twelve to sixteen years, who had taken to sneaking out of their homes and wandering along the county roads before dawn, drinking and making love. One need only recall out of what economic group stem the teenagers and young adults who yearly invade Fort Lauderdale; the Newport Jazz Festival; Astoria, Oregon; and the French Quarter in New Orleans at Mardi Gras time.

As in the case of "decent" language, what the schools consider decent behavior is a myth in American society. The major difference in sexual and drinking behavior among American adolescents is that those of the affluent group make elaborate arrangements to secrete their activities or remain anonymous by joining large groups, while the economically deprived adolescents do neither. As affluent children become adept at knowing when and where to use vulgar language, they learn how to drink and "make out" with minimum chance of discovery. At school, in the formal situation of the classroom, the affluent adolescent is clean and virtuous while between classes in the halls he plots with his buddies his weekend activities. The teacher in her classroom sees and hears agreement with her teachings of right and wrong. Whereas one group makes no bones about what it does, the other continues the process of pretense, giving school what it wants and appearing to be, for politic reasons, what it is not.

4. *Children should talk over their problems rather than fight about them.* Few people can dispute the soundness of this position. It is obviously better to settle differences by reasoning than it is to beat one's adversary bloodily to the ground. It is certainly better for the defeated, and may be better for the victor if the next time he is the one beat. Assuredly this is true as a general rule; convincing by reason is

wiser than fighting. However, perhaps it isn't really too dreadful for two boys to relieve some of their frustrations by ten or fifteen minutes of fisticuffs. The world is full of fast friends who at one time or another were toe to toe. But to fight or not to fight is not the point. As in the case of proper versus improper language, the commandment not to fight provides many an economically deprived child with another reason for further developing his alienation from the public school— and provides another manner in which affluent-oriented teachers can hasten the alienation process. Like it or not, children who grow up in ghetto streets learn to fight. Great prestige is attached to fighting ability. Fathers and older brothers boast of the fighting prowess of a younger child in the family. Many affluent-society fathers do too, but usually when mother is not present and then often adding the admonishment, "But you shouldn't fight, it isn't civilized." Economically deprived children find fighting easier than talking. When words come hard, a punch in the nose is much quicker and more effective in winning an argument.

It is incumbent upon teachers in schools to see that children do not fight. Those in charge of transmitting dominant-society culture must condemn what is unacceptable in this culture. Fighting between two individuals (except in the boxing ring or in organized warfare) is unacceptable. How the child is convinced not to fight, however, is the important issue at hand. When Johnny gets knocked down at recess, usually a predictable series of events follows. He gets up, ready, and though some of his more sophisticated buddies might try to stop him, it's often too late. By the time the teacher arrives at the scene there is a circle of a hundred boys and girls surrounding two in the center, locked in some stage of combat.

The teacher bursts through the group, with little assistance from the assembled, and pulls the two blasphemers apart. The teacher has had a tough day; she has broken up six fights this month; she has fifteen kids who can't read and don't want to; she is ready for Christmas vacation even though it's only the third week in October. She takes hold of Johnny, who has been in three fights since school began a month ago, and screams at him, "How dare you fight! Only animals or savages fight," or "When are you going to learn that nice children don't fight?" or "I'm going to have you suspended till you learn to behave like a decent human being."

One hundred children, many of them economically deprived, to whom fighting is as natural as tossing a ball or pitching pennies, have heard the teacher. Now she is not necessarily prejudiced in the sense that she is overtly hostile to, or does not like, Negro or Puerto Rican children, but she is pushed to the wall; she has a tough job to perform; she is caught in a trap and does not know how to escape. To her, fighting is dead wrong; it is a sign of ignorance and of uncivilized behavior. To her, a fighting child is not a "decent" child. Angry, frustrated, often bitter because of where she has to teach, she gives vent to her feelings and Johnny discovers a strange truth. The boy whom he hit and who hit him back is not his real enemy; the enemy is that woman who has screamed at him and told him that he is no damned good, and by implication, neither is his family. His Dad would be proud of him for defending himself, even though he might admonish him for fighting in school. His older brother would have given him a nickel if he had seen the fight. His friends would kid him later and he'd shadow box in the street and sit on the front steps in the evening and tell lies about how tough he is; and sitting next to him might be the boy he fought with that very afternoon. The teacher's world, the school, principals, tell him and the hundred kids around him that their world is wrong. The alienation process continues.

Does this mean that the teacher should allow children to fight in the school yard? Not at all. It means that the teacher of such children must be a unique kind of human being, able to hide well her true feelings or to genuinely feel there is nothing wrong in two boys fighting. She must break up the fight, because fighting is not tolerated in school, but in doing so she can say, "Boys, I'm going to have to punish you for fighting. You know fighting is not allowed on school grounds. Can you imagine what school would be like if every time someone got angry, a fight started? What you do after three o'clock, after you cross the street and are off the school grounds, is your business. While you are here in school I cannot permit you to fight. I don't approve of your fighting after school or any time, but if you think that's the only way to solve your problem, well you do what you have to do."

This teacher has attacked no value commitment and she has used a logic that almost every child can understand. She has done nothing to indicate that she disapproves of family and friends. She has not equated fighting with savagery, only with behavior expected on school grounds.

How many teachers in the American public schools, working day after day with economically deprived children can be so strong, or are genuinely free from deep-rooted feelings of antagonism toward children whose behavior is so profoundly different from what they have come to accept as correct?

5. *Children should understand the relationship between effort and reward as leading to future success.* Religious leaders proclaim that he who works hard receives blessings. Indeed, the Founding Fathers were men to whom leisure was

the devil's hunting ground. Work today, every day, all day, except Sunday, brought salvation in heaven.

As we in America assume that economic competition is essential to our well-being, we maintain that individual effort leads to reward. The theory that effort leads to reward, in the degree that the effort is exerted, is put forth not as an expression of cultural preference but as a universal truth for man wherever he is. Effort does, in fact, bring reward, but only when a society dictates that it shall, and only in ways prescribed and approved by the society. Among many primitive peoples in the past, and indeed, among many Mexican-Americans today, effort to improve one's lot meets not with reward but with exclusion and condemnation. That hard work or effort brings success or reward is a cultural concept. In a transitional society such as ours, where subcultures are common, there are significant variations, as has been stated, in sets of values of the dominant culture and the various subcultures. Dominant American culture is principally Northwest European in origin, but not all Americans know this. Countless American children, whose parents are not Northwest-European-oriented, and to whom its culture is alien, scarcely understand or believe the assumption made in the public school that effort leads to reward, that is, that one should study his lessons today because this will insure his tomorrow. Indeed, even some Americans whose culture *is* Northwest European in origin have become so far removed from the mainstream of affluent American society, that they no longer understand the relationship between effort and reward.

To be convinced that preparation today will lead to a better tomorrow, one needs to have experienced a good yesterday. In Chekhov's *Uncle Vanya*, Dr. Astrov remarks that to see a small light toward which one may move as he walks through the dense forest is all one needs to keep going, but when there is no light to be seen in the distance, what reason is there for continuing? One may argue with the logic of millions of Americans who believe that there is no light, but it cannot be disputed that their believing it will have serious effects upon their behavior. Belief is truth to the believer. To these millions of Americans the forest is without light, and like Dr. Astrov, children all over America see no reason to continue, or even begin the attempt to leave the forest.

Negro children in the ghettos in South Chicago do not think like the Founding Fathers, nor do the Mexicans in San Antonio, or the Indians on Arizona reservations; neither do the hill-country whites of the Ozarks or Appalachia, though they might be able to trace direct descendency from the Pilgrims. A most poignant example of the denial of effort and reward associations is described by William Madsen. Madsen quotes a Mexican-American of Hidalgo County, Texas, as follows:

> We are not very important in the universe. We are here because God sent us and we must leave when God calls us. God has given us a good way to live and we should try to see the beauty of his commands. We will often fail for many are weak but we should try. There is much suffering but we should accept it for it comes from God. Life is sad but beautiful.[9]

Madsen says of the Mexicans in Hidalgo County:

> Acceptance and appreciation of things as they are constitute primary values of *La Raza*. Because God, rather than man, is viewed as controlling events, the Latin lacks the future orientation of the Anglo and his passion for planning ahead. Many Mexican-Americans would consider it presumptive to try to plan for tomorrow because human beings are merely servants of God and it is He who plans the future.

[9] *The Mexican American of South Texas* (New York: Holt, Rinehart & Winston, Inc., 1964), p. 17.

He is dedicated to living the moment to its fullest in the roles assigned to him by God.[10]

How different is this view from the one accepted in dominant American culture, that if one works hard and presses his advantage, missing no opportunities, he will achieve success. In another section of his work, Madsen states:

> Suffering is also made acceptable by a strong belief in fatalism. It is generally believed that the good or bad fortune of the individual is predestined and every occurrence in human existence comes to pass because it was fated to do so. Fatalistic philosophy produces an attitude of resignation, which often convinces the Anglo that the Latin lacks drive and determination. What the Anglo tries to control, the Mexican-American tries to accept. Misfortune is something the Anglo tries to overcome and the Latin views as fate.[11]

In the lives of many of our economically deprived people the promise of effort-reward is foreign and unacceptable. Children who grow up in ghettos see old, decaying, rat-infested buildings and dirty garbage-strewn streets. In the rural areas of the economically deprived, housing is also substandard, with whole families living in one-room shacks without the most basic facilities that dominant American society considers as elementary needs. In both the ghettos and the impoverished rural areas facilities are primitive and disease-producing. Living in poverty are millions of American men and women who are jobless; countless others work only a portion of the year and then usually at low-paying jobs; many more travel with their families from shack to shack, picking fruit or harvesting cotton or wheat; still others share-crop on

[10] *Ibid.*
[11] *Ibid.*, p. 16.

acreage of insufficient size to insure a minimally adequate income. Their lives of poverty breed resignation and hopelessness. Substandard diet devitalizes and causes aimlessness. Crowded and unsanitary living conditions create unbelievable tensions and anxieties. Lack of proper education perpetuates ignorance. School is a chimera.

All combine to create an environment so different from affluent Americans that to expect the men and women and the children of the economically deprived to think in terms of Horatio Alger is to expect a cultural miracle. Furthermore, besides the misery of poverty, with its concomitant degenerative effects upon all the economically deprived in our society, there is the corroding disease of racial and ethnic prejudice which plays so destructive a part in the life of many of the economically deprived. To the Negro, Puerto Rican, Mexican-American, and Indian comes a second burden: societal rejection because of race. Discrimination, bias, and open hostility reinforce their feelings of inadequacy already created by poverty. Millions of our people forcibly set apart have psychological mind-sets that lead them to distrust affluent America's claim that all people in our country can profit and succeed if only they will apply themselves. Defeated and despised, they deny the sincerity of those who perpetuate the myth; they refuse to accept the possibility of success for themselves and in many cases even take comfort in convincing themselves that the success is not worthwhile. Defenses built up by years of denial and rejection are not easily or quickly broken. It is simpler to accept life as defeating, and to do no more than absolutely necessary to remain alive from day to day, than it is to fight against a seemingly indestructible enemy. James Baldwin refers to the thousands of Negroes in American ghettos who "TV it," that is to say, who have withdrawn from life, work only when it is unavoidably necessary, and sponge on any relatives or friends available. The poor of our country, particularly the colored, have never known success in the lifetime of our nation. Although a certain few are always able to rise above their environment to emerge into the affluent group, the majority are not.

The history of the United States since World War I shows that the Negro, Puerto Rican, and Mexican-American people of our nation have not made the economic and social progress common to other ethnic minority groups. There are sociological reasons for this. The upward social and economic movement of the Irish, Italians, Jews, Greeks, Slavs and other immigrant groups who came to America occurred at a time when our industrial economy was new. Each succeeding wave of immigrants was at first met with hostility. When the Irish, for example, came to our shores in great numbers in the last half of the nineteenth century, they suffered extreme poverty, their crime rate was high, drinking extensive, family life often disjointed and tension-ridden. Within three or four decades, however, the Irish became "Americanized" and were able to find better jobs and more decent housing, and to develop higher levels of aspiration. Work for the unskilled and uneducated was at that time available. That was a time in American history when the rapid growth and development of industry and the railroads made it possible for men with strong backs and uneducated minds to find the job opportunities needed to begin the process of becoming members of the affluent. Another element in the integration of these ethnic groups into American society is something that might be called the "replacement cycle." After the Irish had been here for a number of years, new waves of immigrants from Southeast Europe came along. Now there was a group less educated, less "American," and less skilled, and the relatively established Irish could aspire to something better on the social ladder of American society, for they had been replaced at the bottom step.

In a still-expanding economy, each newly arriving immigrant group served its apprenticeship and time of poverty, ignorance, rejection, and suffering. This period, however, was temporary. Sooner or later, with the advantage of the arrival of still another wave of new immigrants, they could be absorbed into the mainstream of American society.

The Negro, Puerto Rican, and Mexican-American immigrants arrived in another time. They have come to find work when work for the unskilled is hard to find. There is no group in the predictable future to take their place at the bottom. They are at the bottom at a time when American society has lost much of its mobility. It is far more difficult for them to move upward, for they do not possess the education or skills they might use to good advantage, at a time when even among the children of the affluent, competition is severe for admittance into the occupations of high prestige. In addition, they face a problem unknown to the immigrants of the nineteenth century: they are colored (or semicolored). They cannot disappear within American society, for they are quickly recognizable.

Thus, three factors have combined in the United States in the last forty years to produce a far more fixed group of economically deprived than ever known before in our history: First, a great slowdown in the rate of development of new industry and a change in the kinds of personnel needed in the twentieth century. Unskilled workers today find little job opportunity. Second, an ending of the "replacement cycle" that made it possible for each new group of immigrants to look over their shoulders and see the next group coming to relieve them of their lowly station. Third, a skin color that does not wash off and the consequent impossibility of disappearing into ethnically anonymous American society.

For the impoverished Caucasians and Negroes of the South, so meager are the opportunities for gainful employment that they, too, find themselves fixed in a relatively immobile position. If they remain on southern soil, they continue to work land that can scarcely produce enough to keep them alive. If they migrate to northern cities, they merely add to the ghettos and rarely improve their social and economic condition. They, like their ghetto brothers in the North, are unskilled, uneducated, and unprepared.

Hopelessness is a state of mind, created out of weariness, poverty, and failure. For the economically deprived to believe, as our schools tell them they should, that by studying hard today they may become "something" twenty years later is to believe in a fairy-tale world. Especially is this true for the Negro. Perhaps now, with the phenomenal development of the Civil Rights movement and with the emergence of their militant and able leaders, their desires and aspirations for improvement will be strengthened. Perhaps the time will come when the potentialities and capabilities of the Negroes in American society will be more fully realized and utilized. But if this becomes a reality it will not be because of what they have learned in school. Indeed, the time may come when because of their militancy they will have secured the right to better education which, after all, they must have if they are to compete for all categories of jobs. Until such time, however, when the levels of aspiration can be raised through this newly unfolding militancy which is resulting in the awakening of the American conscience, the public school as presently constituted has little to offer the economically deprived Negro.

The Negro child in Harlem today sees young men and older ones, too, adrift, unemployed, rebellious, hanging around the local pool halls and bars. Narcotics are easily available. Drunkenness and sexual promiscuity are common, open, and boasted about. Even among the majority of Negro adults with full-time work, the kind of wages received are often not sufficient to raise a family above subsistence level. Poverty and disease are everywhere, jail and violence, and even death are everyday occurrences. Further, in a great many cases, the mother of the family must also work to augment the low income and the children are left to roam the streets. In many Negro homes the family is strongly matriarchal. In these homes the women dominate and often children living in the same family have different surnames, the issue of fathers other than the one currently in the home. Thus great numbers of Negro children in the ghetto grow up in the remorseless grip of poverty, degradation, and instability. Bitterness develops in them. The concept of effort and reward in such circumstances becomes strangely distorted, at least in traditional American terms. Lacking the environment and experience that indicate that the light at the end of the path can be reached, children easily lapse into the life around them. Their real world is rat-infested apartments, pool halls, violence, defeat, and despair. It is not easy to discover amid all of this a relationship between effort and reward.

Among the Mexican-Americans, both urban and rural, conditions also exist and traditions obtain which make it difficult for the children to see relationship between effort and reward as the public school would like to have it understood. Here, as among the Negroes, the adult models for children to copy are often quite unlike the models that the children of the affluent may learn from. In *La Raza*, Madsen discusses the young Mexican male in his late teens or early twenties, the kind of "older" man that young Mexican boys must emulate.

> Weakness in drinking ability is always humiliating. The true man drinks and drinks frequently and in quantity. Inability to maintain dignity when drinking is absolute proof of weakness as is the refusal to drink.
> A favorite sport of the younger generation is testing the *machismo* of their fellows in a drinking situation. In this

game, it is implicitly understood that hidden accusations and taunts are not serious. They are forgotten on leaving the bar unless some individual has gone too far or is too sensitive. An inebriated male is frequently egged on to make a stand that he cannot defend. His argument is then crushed with a well-turned phrase that is considered a triumph and a moment for hilarity.

Male virility is better proven by direct action than by triumphs in verbal doing. The Latin male does not take his sex life lightly. He regards the female sex as a desirable quantity that exists to be conquered, and he is the conqueror. He is proud of the seductions he chalks up and does not hesitate to point them out to his companions. Seduction is the best proof of manliness. . . .

The Latin thinks of a true man as being proud, self-reliant, and virile. He is jokingly compared to a rooster. Ramon [one of Madsen's informants] observed, "the better man is the one who can drink more, defend himself best, have more sex relations, and have more sons borne by his wife. If unmarried, the better man is the one who has the most girl friends; if married, the one who deceives his wife most."

The Latin wife is expected to show her husband absolute respect and obedience. For a wife to question her husband's orders or decisions is to doubt his intelligence—an unforgivable sin. She does not resent her subordinate role, nor envy the independence of Anglo women. Her role fulfillment is seen in helping her husband to achieve his goals as he sees fit. The Latin wife must never express sorrow or anger at her husband's extramarital activities. It is understood that his sexual adventures will not threaten or weaken his devotion to his family. The Mexican-American wife who irritates her husband may be beaten. She should accept this punishment as deserved. Some wives assert that they are grateful for punishment at the hands of their husbands, for such concerns with shortcomings indicates profound love.

Husband and wife share the joint obligation of teaching their children how to conduct themselves with dignity and honor in any social situation. . . . An "educated" person is one who has been well trained as a social being. Informal education within the family is viewed as more important than formal schooling.[12]

This example of some of the values extant among Mexican-Americans today certainly indicates a great gap between what is expected of children in the affluent-oriented public school and what exists and is expected of them in their real world. It might be said that what Mexican boys and girls should be when adulthood is reached is hardly what the public schools would like them to be.

In *The Grapes of Wrath*, in one of the truly impressive scenes in American fiction, John Steinbeck describes the triumphant return home of Joad after four years in prison. To his people, friends and relatives, he is a hero. He has fought the law and won out in the end because he has returned. Among the Caucasian people of much of the southern rural mountain and prairie southwestern areas, established law and authority are traditional enemies. Violation of law and successful defiance of its minions are cause for rejoicing and boasting. So difficult is it to maintain order in some parts of these sections, that entire counties have only token law enforcement. For this segment of our society, effort and reward may be of value, but not the kind of value the affluent-oriented public school would like to see develop. Mountain children have models to copy which are scarcely approved, at least by the standards of dominant American society. Feuding, moonshining, draft evasion and other unlawful acts are often approved by the elders and, of course, copied by the children.

As to the southern rural Negro, functionally illiterate in most cases and denied even the most elementary democratic rights, it is almost impossible to convince him that effort leads to commensurate reward. (U.S. Census, 1964, shows that 89.7

[12] *Ibid.*, pp. 19-20.

per cent of Negroes in Louisiana over age 25 have not graduated from high school. In some parishes functional illiteracy is as high as 64.5 per cent for both Negro and white.) Weakened by decades of substandard living conditions, frightened by real and vicious enemies, hornswoggled into accepting his fate as inevitable, the southern rural Negro lives from day to day, surviving as best he can in a world in many ways more confusing than it was in the time of slavery.

In our dominant culture, reward for effort is stressed everywhere, but nowhere more than in the public school situation. Margaret Mead has stated that the difference between education in a primitive society and a modern industrial society is that the children in the former learn what they must to be adults, whereas the children in the latter learn what someone thinks they ought to. It is the *ought to* in American public education that causes the difficulty.

We do not prepare our children in school to be adults. Our formal education consists primarily of a series of curriculum offerings the temporary mastery of which leads to the presentation of a tool to open the door to college and, in the majority of cases, to economic success. Children in the public schools do not learn kinship regulations, religion, ritual, fishing, art, hunting, weapon- and tool-making. Our children learn grammar, arithmetic, history, and science. In a primitive society education, whatever form it takes, is based upon deeply imbedded roots of life, the mastery of specific skills crucial for survival as an adult. The child sees these skills in use every day of his life and realizes the need for learning them. He knows, too, that he is threatened with ostracism if he does not learn the social ways of his people.

In American society children do not experience, nor can they sense, that study of history, science, mathematics, or literature is necessary for them to become successful adults. The education world of a primitive child is real. The education world of a child in a complex industrial society is make-believe.

Under these circumstances, motivation for learning obviously presents severe difficulties. Little manufactured motivation is needed to convince a Bushman child that he should learn to hunt. All the healthy adult males in his village hunt. His models are consistent. In our society adult models represent a wide spectrum of behavior. Which model does one follow? How does one become like the model?

The model chosen by the majority of the children of the affluent, though it may vary in form, does not vary greatly in kind, and the path to follow remains basically the same: school, good grades, college prep programs, Cub Scouts, Boy Scouts, Girl Scouts, church groups, student government, the right friends, and so on. For the affluent who do not choose to attend college, apprentice programs and other such skill-producing opportunities are available through father and friends. Long before the cradle the plans are made. From the time of infancy the plan is put into execution. Motivation for the majority of affluent children is based upon the realization that school is the single most important tool for entering the affluent world after proper apprenticeship. Without "learning" and good grades one cannot make it. Many affluent children do not like school but they need it; often they do not like teachers but they need them. They are academically talented because the need to be so is strong and constant. They are academically talented because the pressure to be so overshadows all else in their young lives. Efforts which lead to good grades lead to affluence, good marriage, and social position.

What of the other children in American society? What kind of motivation for formal education do they have? As has been pointed out, ghetto children or impoverished children have different kinds of models to copy, and other paths to follow. Whereas success among the affluent is measured by more affluence, success among the poor—not by choice, but by necessity—often takes on other forms. The poor find other ways to achieve prestige and status among themselves. To these children growing up in a rough, raw, and physically demanding world, study and formal learning become sissified pursuits. Whom can they point to in their world who gained anything worthwhile from going to school?

In a society such as ours, where entire groups of people are summarily rejected, the rejected in turn build a wall to cut themselves off from the rejectors. In a community that denies the worth of many of its members, those considered worthless will so consider the community. The pressures upon the rejected children to join in the fight against the outside world are strong. Ghetto children of the economically deprived who do well in school become suspect among their own. Those who appear to want to move in the "other" kind of life may be called "white Niggers," or worse. If they accept the school and its values they do so at the risk of ostracism by their street mates. The school is an enemy and in most cases so is the teacher; they represent the hostile world and must be opposed. The ghetto says to its children, "Do not deceive yourselves into believing what 'they' say, that you can amount to something if you want to, because in Uncle Charlie's world or the Anglo's world you are nothing."

In their appraisal that school has little value for them, the children of the economically deprived are essentially correct. School has not been very kind to them. The process of alienation is powerful. Society alienates and rejects the economically deprived. And the school is society's agent. Not to understand and abide by the myth of effort and reward is to commit the cardinal sin in the public school. How many times in America has a second-grade teacher remarked: "If only they would help themselves. I can't do anything with them until they do."

How many times have third-grade teachers said: "They don't care anything about school or learning. They're either stupid or lazy." How many times have fourth-grade teachers said: "This school isn't what it used to be. You should have seen it before *they* came."

What the teachers say is true. The children of the poor most often do not help themselves as far as school is concerned; they do change the face of a school when they are bussed in or given access to a non-ghetto school in some other way. Ghetto children are lazy and do act stupidly in school situations. The alienation of the children by the school results in the rejection by the children of the school. Our society alienates the economically deprived and in turn they reject the society. Hard work in school may bring reward to some, but it is not what the children of the poor can expect. It is outside of their living experience and that of their parents as well.

FOUR

Curriculum for
the economically deprived

Despite their distrust of the school, and in the face of ongoing alienation, some of the economically deprived children do manage to remain in high school until they graduate. Although it is difficult to determine just how many of the children of the poor today will finish school, or have done so in the past ten years, it would certainly be safe to say that fewer do than don't. Those who graduate do so largely in the hope that a diploma will help them attain a better place within even the limited job opportunities traditionally open to them (particularly the non-Caucasians) in American society. However, they are scarcely better off for completing the ordeal of high school. In most cases the curriculum offered them is poorly planned, academically weak, and basically uncoordinated, with the result that few graduates are equipped with saleable skills. The majority of the children of the poor

73

have been placed in the nonacademic programs, particularly in high school. They have been routed through watered-down elementary and junior high school programs. The reading ability among great numbers of these children in high school is far below their grade level, and in some cases almost non-existent; mathematics has been limited to simple arithmetic; geography and other social sciences are almost entirely neglected; science consists of the most basic elementary material, and in many cases is not included in the curriculum beyond the ninth grade. Indeed, many of the so-called slow learners in the American public schools never have an opportunity to do any kind of laboratory work in science. Literature consists of the most sterile kind of pap, even in high school. Many of the economically deprived children have never heard of Dickens, Hemingway, Shaw, and so on, much less had an opportunity of becoming even remotely familiar with their writings. The woodshop, metal shop and machine shop courses, given in abundance to the economically deprived in high school, are generally remarkably unrelated to the development of specific skills and, because of the poor reading achievement of the students, are of necessity academically weak. For the daughters of the economically deprived, the absence of academic subject matter is also common in high school. Instead of shop courses the girls' programs often consist of typing, business mathematics, clerical practice, chorus, homemaking, and so on. Rarely do they even take stenography, much less the traditional academic subjects.

Ironically, all is done by design. These children are deliberately channeled into weak nonacademic programs. The explanation for this procedure lies in the all-embracing phrase that has become so fashionable in the vocabulary of educationists: "We meet the individual needs of every child. Since it is well known that the economically deprived are generally slow learners, have poor I.Q.'s, are academically untalented, and lack motivation, it would be a disservice to give them an academic education. Their needs would not be met. All of our latest scientific knowledge indicates that these children tend to be nonverbal, therefore poorly equipped for school. By placing them in the slower, general and vocational program tracks we avoid the necessity of failing them and forcing them to quit school."

Despite the sincerity of many who adhere to this thinking and in the name of benefiting the child, we turn him out of high school, if he manages to finish, semiliterate, unlettered, and unskilled. From the first grade to the twelfth, the economically deprived children, under the blanket of psychometric and psychological jargon, are denied meaningful opportunity by the American public schools as their parents have been by American society. Again, it must be emphasized that as reflectors of our society, our public schools are merely giving us what we have asked for.

To be sure, in recent years some school districts have spent considerable money, time, and effort in establishing special programs to upgrade and intensify the academic education of economically deprived children. However, as commendable as these attempts are, the efforts have been so few and far between and the numbers of children affected so minimal that in no way can these isolated examples of concern leading to action be considered as a reversal of trend.

Let us look at a study[1] made of the economically deprived population in an integrated high school in one of the most up-to-date school facility areas in the United States, the Bay Area of California. This school is located within fifty miles of two of the leading teacher-training institutions in the United

---

[1] Nathaniel Hickerson, "Participation by Negroes and Non-Negroes in the Formal and Informal Activities of a California High School," Unpublished dissertation, University of California, Berkeley, 1962.

States, the University of California and Stanford University. At both of these institutions, research in education is of a high order. These universities furnish much of California with its superintendents and principals.

The high school is a typically ethnically integrated school, an hour's commuting distance from San Francisco. The purpose of the study was to determine the kinds of formal and informal activities entered into by Negro, Mexican-American, Filipino and Caucasian students in the school population, which groups comprised more than 99 per cent of the total attendance. The 888 students used in the sample (167 Negro, 118 Mexican-American, 44 Filipino, and 559 Caucasian) were examined in order to ascertain the following information: what percentage of each ethnic group was assigned to the academically fast sections of English; what percentage of each group was assigned to college preparatory, secretarial, clerical, and general program tracks; what percentage of each group participated in what kinds of clubs, and social and interscholastic activities.

With the aid of the staff in the offices of the local industries, together with available school records, the occupations of the fathers of the students were traced and classified as professional, executive, semi-executive, business, skilled, semiskilled, unskilled, and unemployed. Finally, on the basis of data gathered from the school records, the students were divided into quartiles according to I.Q. scores. Comparisons were made among the four ethnic groups in the school.

Comparisons of the children whose fathers were employed as executives, semi-executives, or professionals, or who owned their own businesses could not be made. Only four Negroes and five Mexican-Americans had fathers who qualified for these categories. The major portion of the study, therefore, concerned itself with comparisons among students whose fathers were skilled and semiskilled workers. The data that are of greatest interest here concern the sons and daughters of the unskilled, unemployed, and welfare recipients in the community. The figures show that a total of 148 children of unskilled workers and unemployed welfare recipients were enrolled in the high school. Eighteen (12.2 per cent) were in the accelerated sections of English. Of the 740 students whose fathers were at least semiskilled workers, 346 (46.8 per cent) were in the accelerated sections of English. Only 13 (8.8 per cent) of the children of the economically deprived were college preparatory students, while 312 (42.2 per cent) of the other group were college preparatory students. Among the children of the economically deprived, 111 (75 per cent) were general majors, that is, graduating from high school (if they made it) with little academic preparation and no discernible skills. Among the children of the affluent, 266 (36 per cent) were general majors.

Conversations with school counselors revealed that at least 40 per cent as many children as those in school at the time of the study had dropped out within the previous four years. No records were available by which to determine how many more of the children of the unskilled and unemployed had dropped out of high school before this study was made.

Further investigation revealed the following: of the 148 children of the economically deprived, 14 (9.5 per cent) had studied a foreign language. Among the children of the affluent, 264 (35.7 per cent) had studied a foreign language. Of the 85 juniors and seniors whose fathers were unskilled or unemployed, 6 (7.1 per cent) had taken chemistry and 4 (4.7 per cent) had been assigned to second year algebra. Of the 423 juniors and seniors whose fathers were in the affluent group, 154 (36.4 per cent) had enrolled in chemistry and 106 (25 per cent) were in or had taken second year algebra. Of the 40 seniors whose fathers were unskilled or unemployed, 1 (2.5 per cent) was enrolled in physics and 1 (2.5 per cent) in chemistry. Of the 224 seniors with affluent parents, 60 (26.7 per cent) were in physics and 25 (11.1 per cent) were in trigonometry.

Harold Hodgkinson has pointed out that the economic position of family is a most significant criterion for determining the kind of a high school education a child may receive in the American public schools. He states:

> If you know the income and occupation of a student's father, you can predict whether or not he will go to college almost as well as you could by using intelligence test scores. . . . The school program is geared largely to the needs of those who come from good environments and are *bound* to be successful.[2]

One other set of figures is pertinent at this point. It has been shown that 75 per cent of the children of the unskilled and unemployed were in the general program track and 8.8 per cent were college preparatory. Of the remaining 16.2 per cent, all girls, 14.1 per cent were clerical majors taking such courses as typing, business mathematics, business English, and clerical practice, and only 2.1 per cent were secretarial students enrolled in the much more difficult and skill-producing courses such as stenography and office practice. In the group of the children of the affluent, there were 22 per cent who were not college preparatory or general majors. Of this 22 per cent only 7 per cent were clerical majors, while 15 per cent were secretarial students enrolled in the more difficult classes. Even among the girls classified as business majors, differentiation was in marked evidence between those whose fathers were unskilled and unemployed, and those whose fathers were members of the affluent.

Again it should be emphasized that these data apply only

---

[2] *Education in Social and Cultural Perspectives* (Englewood Cliffs, N.J.: Prentice-Hall, Inc., 1961), p. 86.

to students enrolled in the school at the time the study was made in 1962. Many children of the unskilled and unemployed had already dropped out of high school, and undoubtedly the largest percentage of these had been enrolled in the slower English sections and the general program track. If their numbers were to be added to the children in school receiving relatively unusable curricula, the conclusion can be only too obvious. A large majority of the children of the unemployed and unskilled in this community, in one of the most progressive parts of the United States, are getting the kind of training from school that provides them with practically nothing to offer future employers.

It is interesting to note that in this school, I.Q. scores are evidently not significant in determining pupils' ability to do college prep work if other factors, such as motivation, are in operation. Review of I.Q. scores indicated that among the affluent the average score in the tenth grade was 100.4. For the children of the economically deprived it was 93.6. Among the 44 Filipino students, however, all of whose fathers were career military personnel either active or retired and were therefore considered affluent, the average I.Q. score was only 92.7. Despite this score, somewhat more than 50 per cent of the Filipino children were college prep or secretarial majors, and almost all of them were doing relatively well in their studies. It must be concluded that motivation, whatever its cause, is, at least in this case, far more important in determining academic success than a so-called measure of native intelligence.

It may be added that the best information available indicated that during the previous twelve to fifteen years no more than two or three of the two hundred or so high-school graduates who were children of the unskilled or unemployed succeeded in graduating from college. Some twenty to thirty more started junior college but few of them continued beyond the first semester, or at best, first year. During the same period hundreds of the sons and daughters of the affluent had graduated from college, and more than a thousand had begun.

Finally, it should be noted that the community is not a blighted area; it is one of the most prosperous industrial communities in the East Bay area of San Francisco, with financial assets that make it possible to afford one of the highest ratios of money per student available to the schools in all of California.

The data uncovered in this study obtain practically everywhere in the United States. In Los Angeles, for example, which has a Mexican population larger than any other city in the world except Mexico City, 74 per cent of the students with Spanish surnames leave high school before graduation. In other southwestern cities even greater percentages of the Mexican-American students leave school before graduation.[3] In Louisiana, as previously mentioned, 89.7 per cent of all Negroes over 25 years of age are non-high-school graduates, and 57.2 per cent of all whites over 25 are also school dropouts. Study after study indicates that everywhere in the United States the children of the poor in great numbers do not finish school, or if they do, it is with few saleable skills. Although a few scattered efforts have been made in various cities to extend some semblance of academic education to the academically deprived, these attempts are not much more than window dressing. For every one economically deprived student enrolled in an experimental academically oriented program, there are a thousand children of the poor who have no such opportunity.

[3] James E. Alitas, "Our Own Language Barrier," *American Education* (Washington, D.C.: U.S. Department of Health, Education, and Welfare, January 1965), pp. 12, 13.

FIVE

The grand design

The preceding chapters have described the process by which the children of the economically deprived in our society are systematically set apart by the institution of the American public schools so that they receive little or no preparation for admittance into the affluent world when they reach adulthood.

In the first and second grades the children are labeled slow readers because they bring with them few skills from home. They are then consigned to slow reading groups, in which the material is kept at a low level. By the third or fourth grades, after two years of presumably learning to read, these children have acquired a reading vocabulary far below that of the children in the fast groups. It is at this point that the children are given I.Q. or other standardized tests and on the basis of low scores achieved—primarily because of lack of reading ability, low morale, poor motivation, and language difficulties—are pronounced slow learners. From this point on the children are destined to receive low-level academic instruction in all phases of the curriculum. By the time the children have finished the fifth and sixth grades, they will have been subjected to years of impoverished schooling, and the likelihood is that their reading levels are now so low that it would be impossible to conceive of their pursuing a rigorous curriculum.

By the time these children reach junior high school they are far behind not only in reading but in writing, arithmetic, science, geography, and history. Their weak academic program continues, only now they are falling farther and farther behind because their work in the seventh and eight grades is scarcely better than it was in the third and fourth. When they are "ready" for high school, the high schools are faced with the problem of deciding what to do with them. To be sure, in junior high school they have "studied" the academic subjects, but the courses have been geared to children reading third- and fourth-grade-level books. It takes an extraordinary teacher to be able to impart a curriculum to children age fourteen or fifteen who have reading vocabularies of two or three hundred words.

A typical ninth-grade program for economically deprived boys consists of a slow English class where a complete sentence written by a child is considered phenomenal; a science course that often offers no experience in a laboratory and uses textbooks written for elementary-grade children; a social studies class that in many cases busies itself with the problems of how to groom well, how to act on a date, how to drive a car, and how to become oriented to the high school building, more than with history or geography. Even when history and geography are taught, the low-level reading ability of the children sharply limits what can be accomplished. A math class reaches its zenith when one-third of the children have learned how to add fractions. Finally, the boys take physical education and probably a shop course.

For the girls of the economically deprived the curriculum is basically the same, with the substitution of homemaking for shop.

In the tenth grade these same students are offered English via such literature as *Popular Mechanics*, "How I Won My Drag Race," or a thin gruel concocted out of *Tom Sawyer*. Rarely, if ever, are these children offered anything that even faintly resembles literature of depth and value. There may be a class of world history, usually not, and if so it is again severely limited because of the inability of many of the students to read anything other than the most elementary material. Essay tests or written reports are out of the question. How can children be expected to fulfill such tasks when their spelling is so deficient and the ability to write complete sentences is beyond them?

In many schools mathematics and science end at the ninth grade for those in the nonacademic program tracks. The boys fill in their programs with shop courses, the girls with typing, more homemaking, glee club, and so on. The junior and senior years for these adolescents are similar to the sophomore year. Typical of a senior boy's program are English (the same quality as in the ninth grade, and about the same quality as the fifth grade); metal shop; machine shop; physical education; study hall (Heaven knows what for); and chorus. In the states that require problems of American democracy in the senior year, this is given in place of one of the other offerings. Needless to say, once again the lack of reading ability seriously hampers depth learning.

For the girls, business English is substituted for English and clerical office practice (not shorthand), drama, and glee club for the shops. It does not matter whether a traditional

84 *The grand design*

subject matter curriculum is the answer to the question of how we should educate children. What is important is that, at present, without this preparation chances for economic success are sharply reduced. The completion of the subject-matter-oriented curriculum provides the key to entrance into the affluent world. Children who do not acquire the key find the doors to economic success locked to them.

High school is now completed. For every one economically deprived student who completes even this program and graduates, there is more than likely one who drops out of school before his twelve-year sentence is up. Millions of American children are thus made ready to face life and supposedly find economic opportunities—semiliterate, unskilled, and totally lacking in commitment to any form of intellectual function, whether they have graduated or not.

It must be repeated that not only is the curriculum woefully inadequate for the economically deprived, but the difficulties of the children in receiving some kind of meaningful formal education are compounded by other factors at work in the school. Chief among these are the attitudes of teachers toward these children. In many elementary school districts where homogeneous grouping is practiced, teachers are rotated from classroom to classroom from year to year. If, for example, there are three fourth-grade classes and one is established as a slow group, then once every three years one of the fourth-grade teachers is assigned her "tough duty" year. She is rewarded the other two years by assignment to the brighter classes. It is a year of penance for most of the teachers faced with the tough class: patience is tried, morale is low, frustration is deep, and the children suffer as the teacher suffers. Lack of cooperation and understanding is all too common. The year is somehow survived, with the teachers often totally unable to reach the children, serving instead as baby sitters or policemen. It goes without saying, these slow, tough classes are made up chiefly of the economically deprived.

In other elementary schools the new teachers, fresh out of college, are assigned to serve their apprenticeship by teaching the lower economic group of children. Here tenure brings reward; the longer a teacher remains in such a school, the greater her chance of being assigned to the "teachable" children. To the inexperienced, neophyte teacher is left the task of doing something with the "dummies." (Perhaps this may be an advantage to the children, since among the young teachers cynicism and low morale have not yet had time to set in.) Unfortunately, however, as most of our teacher-training institutions do little to prepare new teachers for working with the economically deprived, their lack of knowledge and understanding often causes serious problems. Their initial good intentions are spoiled by poor execution; willingness, while highly desirable, is not enough if skill and understanding are lacking. When the new teacher of a slow class complains, "I can't do a thing with them," she is frequently told by the principal and other teachers alike, "Well, what do you expect? Do the best you can. You can't make nuclear physicists out of a bunch of 73 I.Q.'s." Loss of initial enthusiasm, drudgery, and ensuing low morale are typical occupational hazards for the elementary teacher assigned to the "slow" children.

It is not to be inferred that all elementary teachers react in this negative way. Some of the finest teaching is done by those who work with the "slow." Indeed, some of these teachers are looked upon as having accomplished the impossible when the slow children in their care—supposedly almost incapable of learning—begin to show interest in school and much higher levels of accomplishment than ever before. A word in education jargon has even been coined to explain this phenomenon. We speak of these children as "overachievers." Their standardized test scores and previous teachers' observations have prognosticated low ability. Imagine the surprise when under careful guidance and sympathetic understanding these children begin to put to the lie the decisions made earlier about them.

The good teachers for the so-called slow children, however, are all too rare. The public school institution in American society is not interested in the prejudged slow student. If it were, there would not be millions of semiliterate young American men and women living in every state of the Union, unable even to begin to compete with their educated peers for the available jobs. The tragedy, unfortunately, is that the neglected students are almost without fail culled from among the families of the economically deprived. One need not consult carefully prepared statistics, but need only look around to see how many young adults from affluent families in American society are unable to read, how many do not have all kinds of job opportunities, how many have dropped out of high school or have failed to graduate because they were discipline problems and were therefore excluded, how many go on to college. Then look around at the numbers of young adults of the economically deprived who cannot read or whose reading ability is so low as to be of little functional value to them, how many have status jobs available to them even if they have managed to graduate from high school, how many have left school long before graduation or have been excluded because of their behavior, or how many even think about going to college. If one is realistic, the conclusion is inescapable that the public schools in American society have not in the past three or four decades been concerned with what happens to the children of the poor.

As in the case of the elementary school, the indifferent or even hostile attitudes of some teachers toward the academically slow in junior high and high school are clearly discernible. When departmentalization begins, as it usually does in our schools in the seventh grade, it is no longer necessary to assign one instructor to the less able students. Now each teacher with five or six classes a day has his program arranged so that he gets cream as well as rhubarb. A typical program in departmentalized schools with homogeneous grouping calls for a teacher to have one or two fast classes, one or two average classes, and one or two slow classes each day. In this way the "burden" is shared. Each teacher needs suffer but one period, or at most two a day, with the "uneducable." One of the most common of all topics of conversation in the faculty lounge centers around the commiserating of the instructors over their classes of "stupes." The mutual society of denigration and hostility meets every day and among some of the teachers who are angry, anxious, and frustrated by having constantly to face these children, the high point of the work day comes when they can sit down, grab a cup of coffee, light a cigarette, and tell their colleagues of their woes in the slow classes. It need not be emphasized that the time spent with these adolescents is served with as little expenditure of effort and interest as possible. To teach high school students who can barely read or write is indeed a trial—for the students as well as the teacher.

In recent years a startling innovation has been put into practice, particularly in the high schools, which underlines a scarcely believable attitude on the part of the public school institution toward the "slow" academic students. It has become the practice in many high schools all over America to give no student in slow sections a grade higher than C. The reasoning behind this is simple: the children in the fast classes who work hard in a highly competitive arena may merit only a C because of the keenness of the competition, while children in the "slow" classes who do not seem to work hard, could conceivably earn a B because the standards are so much lower. Obviously it is not fair to give a B for a little effort in a low-standard classroom and a C for a great deal of effort in a high-expectancy classroom. Certainly, the student receiving C in a fast section knows more of his particular subject than the student getting B in a slow section. Ergo, children in the slow sections are to be given a grade no higher than C so that the children in the fast classes will not be penalized. It should not be difficult to envision the stimulus for motivation of high school students in "slow" classes when they KNOW THAT NO MATTER HOW HARD THEY WORK THEIR MAXIMUM GRADE WILL BE C.

In schools where homogeneous grouping based upon ability is not practiced, the "slow" often suffer no less than they do in their homogeneous groups. Here the great effort of teachers is most often spent on working with the more able students, on the assumption that little can be done with the slow in high school. It is far better to reach the reachable than to worry about those who do not care or who cannot make it. As John Niemeyer states:

> Our hypothesis is that the chief cause of the low achievement of children of alienated groups is the fact that too many teachers and principals honestly believe that these children are educable only to an extremely limited extent, and when teachers have a low expectation level for their children's learning, the children seldom exceed that expectation, which is a self-fulfilling prophecy.[1]

It is to be expected that a teacher will spend his greatest energy and concentration upon those children who react posi-

---

[1] "Some Guidelines to Desirable Elementary School Reorganization" in *Programs for the Educationally Disadvantaged*, U.S. Office of Education Bulletin No. 17 (1963), p. 81.

tively to his teaching; it is more rewarding to work with them. On the other hand, it is frustrating and disturbing to attempt to accomplish desired ends by teaching the curriculum to those who "don't have it." But how remarkable it is that, for one reason or another, it is almost always the children of the affluent who "have it," while the children of the economically deprived are the ones who "don't have it." If one would argue with the conclusion that this is the assumption made by American public schools, he need only look at Americans to confirm it.

It should be repeated here that the public schools in America, as in every modern country, are protectors and carriers of the existing social and economic order in the society where they are found. American society has apparently decided that it does not need the economically deprived to be anything other than they are. The release of millions of these people into the stream of affluent society would bring about problems of displacement in the economic structure. We are in a time of delicate balance; comparative affluence can be maintained for only four-fifths of our people. There are not enough jobs now, and with automation in industry looming greater and greater as a replacer of men, the situation is not promising. As Christopher Jencks states:

> First, there is no prospect of creating enough well-paid jobs to absorb all of America's children, even if they all earn Ph.D.'s. Mechanization and automation are proceeding extremely fast, and official statistics show that despite the economy's growth, it actually takes fewer workers today than in 1957 to satisfy private demands for goods and services. In recent years, growth of the job market has been produced entirely by government expenditures for things like missiles, highways, education (and the war on poverty), and by the growth of non-profit organizations. Today, however, President Johnson is trying to reduce federal expenditures. Who, then,

is going to hire the children of the poor, even assuming they are well educated? [2]

Four-fifths of our people are substantial, tax-paying members of their communities. Their children will, in most cases, inherit the jobs of their fathers. Belonging to an affluent family in modern America provides great opportunity for achieving economic success and security. By contrast, for the vast majority of those born of the economically deprived, there may be a frightening future ahead. Their children may grow up in a hostile society that, in the past thirty years, has shown little need of them. In San Antonio, Los Angeles, Chicago, Washington, New York, New Orleans, Birmingham, and hundreds of other cities, the children of the poor may, as all too often in the past, grow up to be poor. In Kentucky, Mississippi, Maine, and 47 other states the children of the disadvantaged may, as all too often in the past, grow up to be disadvantaged. One may look proudly at fine new suburban high schools in Westchester County, New York, but one had better look at the schools in "Mexican" San Antonio as well.

[2] "Speaking Out," *Saturday Evening Post*, March 13, 1965, p. 14.

SIX

Proposals for reform

Any program or series of programs designed to correct the inequalities of opportunity available to our economically deprived children in the public schools can only be undertaken in conjunction with profound changes in our culture. As the schools are reflective of society, so it follows that for the image to change, the face looking in the mirror must be altered. The schools cannot provide economically deprived children with jobs, decent housing, or social acceptance. The schools cannot motivate the unmotivated. The schools cannot alter the mores and traditions of a whole people. All that our schools can do is to give us what we want. A society gets what it wants, and if at present we want nearly one-fifth of our people to live in such "poverty pockets" as rural Louisiana, Harlem, Appalachia, the San Joaquin Valley of California, and others, our schools will follow the mandate to prolong them. If at present ours is a race culture, committed to social inequality, then our schools will turn out children to fit this requirement.

Change, when it comes, will emerge in the form of a serious reconsideration in American society of the role of each individual. As we truly come to believe that every child is uniquely capable in his own way, and can mature to be of service to himself and his society, then will our schools develop the knowledge and exhibit the desire to meet the *new* requirements placed upon them by a demanding society. But in no way does this mean that we in public education must sit back and say, "We can do nothing until all around us changes clearly, irrevocably, and unmistakably." For change is subtle and can pass almost unnoticed unless one has an eye warily cocked. There is a spirit in our land today that is new and fresh and above all crying to be understood. There has developed among our people in the last decade more awareness of the plight of our poor and rejected than in the 180 years that preceded it. Law and custom have been drastically altered all about us. Upheaval, anger, turmoil, open rebellion have signified new demands for social and economic opportunity. We have much to do and we will not erase overnight what has been produced by time and commitment; yet in America today, change is everywhere. Societies cling to the past, but we are moving faster now than ever before in the direction of recognizing fundamental and basic problems in the construction of a new and vital American society that is truly egalitarian and democratic.

In such a setting it is possible—rather, *imperative*—that our public schools read the signs and join the fight. Always before, our institution of public education has carried out the demands placed upon it. Always before, our schools have been able to make decisions as to what could *now* be done in light of changing conditions. There is no need for the public schools suddenly to reverse their traditional role and become reconstructionist (if, indeed, they ever could). On the contrary,

what our public education institution must do is correctly
interpret and act upon what has now gained credence in our
society: After nearly two hundred years the "American dream"
still has not been fulfilled—and it must be if we are to survive
in a politically and economically hostile world.

Though the public schools cannot create jobs, they can
produce adults who possess the skills to compete for them.
Though the public schools cannot smash housing restriction
covenants and destroy ghettos, they can produce adults who
do not like covenants and ghettos and who are willing to say
so whether they suffer from them directly or as spectators.
Though the public schools cannot end racial, ethnic, or religious bigotry, they can help to build among their charges
decent attitudes toward people who are different. Though the
public schools cannot erase all the conditions that produce
feelings of worthlessness among children, they can work long
and diligently to create conditions in the school environment
that help children along the way toward dignity and self-
appreciation. Our schools can do these things now because for
the first time in our history America has given its blessing to
such a monumental undertaking.

It would be presumptuous to suggest that there is a way
to finish the task. Since we have scarcely begun, it is impossible to foresee how we will get to where we wish to go if,
indeed, we arrive there at all. But some things we must do,
and quickly:

1. *Produce teachers who have had thorough exposure to
psychological, sociological, and anthropological theory and
data concerning the relationship between race and intelligence
and the effect of culture upon behavior.* It is impossible to
expect teachers to understand behavior of children who are

"different" unless they are allowed to come in contact with contemporary thought about race and intelligence, culture and behavior.

2. *Insist that our future teachers be provided by teacher-training institutions with varied experiences in working with the children of the economically deprived.* At present, many future teachers are allowed to complete their student teaching in public schools where only the children of the affluent are in attendance. Many of these teachers then are expected to enter the profession ready for assignment to any school regardless of the socio-economic background of its students. It is unfair to expect the teacher who has had little or no experience with the economically deprived to become a successful teacher of them. It is unfair as well to subject children to a teacher who, because of lack of concrete experience, is unable to appreciate their behavior based on particular cultural tradition.

3. *Deny entry into the teaching profession to all those who are not reasonably free of race-mindedness or social or economic caste-inspired intolerance.* As we insist that our teachers should be academically prepared to teach their subject matter effectively, so we must insist that these same teachers not harm the children of the economically deprived through behavior based upon hostility and arrogance bred of feelings of superiority. (If this is a difficult task, consider the result if we do *not* exclude the intolerant from the teaching profession. Enter any one of thousands of public schools today and see the results of the presence of race- and caste-minded teachers.)

4. *Weed out of the teaching profession those already in it whose attitudes toward children are warped because of race*

or class bias. State legislatures and boards of education should make indications of bigotry on the part of teachers grounds for dismissal as violation of state law and board policy. If some would suggest that this is unfair to teachers presently employed, consider what it is to the children in their care. Instead of weeding out the children, as we have all too often done in the past, perhaps we should think about removing some of the teachers and saving more of the children.

5. *Alter our curriculum in the social sciences so as to indicate to our children that democracy can be truly raceless and casteless.* Our present textbooks in the social sciences are for the most part totally inadequate. Little or no information in the past has been available in these books to inspire minority-group children with pride in the contributions of *their* people to the development of American society. Recently some efforts have been made to correct this condition. We must continue the work just begun until our textbooks give adequate coverage to the significant roles played by minority groups in the development of American society. As well, there is a serious lack of integration of disciplines in the social sciences. Few of our children in the public schools are permitted to read, study, and learn about race and intelligence, culture and behavior. Even fewer are allowed to discuss frankly the nature and origins of prejudice and hate. If we hope to produce democratic-minded people, it behooves us to give them some cement into which to jam the pilings.

6. *Eliminate I.Q. testing as a means of determining innate intelligence in children.* After fifty or more years of strenuous effort and great expense, we are no closer today than we ever were to producing tests that measure inborn intelligence as something separate from learning, experience, and environment. Indeed, a major contribution of I.Q. and

related tests in public schools has been to justify our removal of the children of the economically deprived from the mainstream of public education. If we are truly interested in getting these children back where they belong, then it would be reasonable to assume that we should do away with the devices that have been most instrumental in setting them apart.

7. *Examine carefully our practices of grouping children according to supposed ability.* It need not be emphasized again how much of this grouping has been based in the past upon personal biases of teachers, faulty measuring devices, and general expectancies that have arisen as a result of race and caste consciousness.

8. *Make tireless efforts to bring the families of the economically deprived into the school environment as active participants.* Constant and continued pressure must be brought to bear upon parents to encourage their children to do well in school, provide them with work space at home when available, use tutoring service when possible, and take advantage of the host of new programs like Operation Headstart to increase the chances of their children's school success. We have assumed for far too long that the majority of the economically deprived parents are not concerned with their children in school. Show these parents genuine interest, exhibit concern as we have so often failed to do in the past, and "miracles" may take place.

9. *Bring into our schools those representatives of minority groups and economically deprived peoples who have achieved economic success.* The presence of professional men, businessmen, athletes, actors, and others, who themselves were at one time disadvantaged, can have a profound effect upon the children of the economically deprived and

their concept of an adult model. Continuous involvement of these successful men in the curriculum of the school can present an ongoing picture of what one can become. (Hopefully, our society will allow for greater numbers of these examples in the future.) Many children of the affluent might also benefit from the experience of viewing successful members of minority groups occupying far different roles than they had been led to expect.

10. *Enlist the aid of the older children of the economically deprived who have done well in school and who are now in the last years of high school.* These high-school-aged youngsters should be encouraged to go into the elementary classrooms and talk with the younger children about the value of school. Again, not only will this be of value to the children of the economically deprived, but it may also have a salutory effect upon the children of the affluent.

11. *Substantially strengthen the academic curriculum offered to economically deprived children.* For those now in school, nationwide remedial programs affecting *all* of these children should be instituted. Class sizes must be drastically reduced, hopefully to ratios of ten or twelve to one. The most effective, understanding teachers should be encouraged to teach the children most needing them. Incentives such as reduced class sizes, teachers' aides, increased salaries, and use of the newest equipment should be provided for the teachers of the economically deprived so as to attract a greater number of the more proficient teachers into this activity.

12. *Continue the process of the desegregation of schools and complete it as quickly as possible.* As long as our schools are segregated, through whatever cause, loss of opportunity is inevitable. The doctrine of "separate but equal" is totally

antithetical to the most basic democratic thinking and acts as one of the strongest forces in creating feelings of rejection among the segregated and feelings of superiority among the dominant.

13. *Institute massive in-service education programs concerned with the education of the economically deprived for teachers, administrators, and counselors now engaged in public school work.* Large numbers of American teachers are genuinely concerned with difficulties involved in teaching the children of the economically deprived. Unfortunately, many of them have never been afforded the opportunity to learn how to translate their concern into positive action. Well-planned and thorough in-service programs, utilizing experts in the field of the education of the economically deprived, may do a great deal toward helping these conscientious teachers become better equipped to face their children.

If it can be argued that many of these programs will cost great sums of money, it can be answered that no amount of expense that we now enter into could possibly make up for the exorbitant waste of human talent and energy that has plagued us in the past. If our nation can spend nearly 75 billion dollars a year for defense, surely we can afford the monies needed to give to millions of our children a hope for the future their parents never had.

If we are truly serious about extending to *all* in our nation the opportunity to prosper, we can afford to wait no longer. We must mobilize all of our resources, abilities, and ingenuity in a massive effort to rectify the wrongs that have come about as part of the growing pains in the development of a great society. Society and school, one and the same, must now show what they can do. In America, people come first, *all* people.